REA

Outdoor Navigation
with GPS

Outdoor Navigation with GPS

Stephen W. Hinch

 **ANNADEL PRESS**
Santa Rosa, California

Printed in the United States of America

First Printing, May 2004

10 9 8 7 6 5 4 3 2 1

Annadel Press, P.O. Box 9398, Santa Rosa, CA 95405
http://www.annadelpress.com

Library of Congress Control Number 2004090302
ISBN 0-9661999-3-6

Cover Photos: Grand Tetons and Snake River by Steve Hinch; eTrex Vista courtesy of Garmin International
Cover design by Greg Hinch

Warning

Information in this book is accurate to best of the author's knowledge at the time of publication. Author and publisher assume no liabilities for damages arising from errors, omissions, or misleading information in this book, regardless of cause. You must always take responsibility for your own health and safety in any outdoor endeavor. This book is no substitute for your GPS receiver's instruction manual, nor does it teach all you should know about survival situations. Before attempting any outdoor activity, be sure you have the background, knowledge, and hands-on training necessary for the task, and you are properly equipped. If these conditions are not satisfactory, you may return this book unread for a full refund.

To Juliana, Greg, and Nicki

Acknowledgments

This book grew from a love of the wilderness—those regions the author Edward Abbey called the "back of beyond." As such, I must acknowledge not only those who contributed directly to its writing, but also the friends who encouraged me through shared adventures in the outdoors.

I first thank my wife Nicki, who not only tolerated my many hours at the keyboard writing yet another book, but also proofread every page. It was she who originally discovered geocaching and thereby found a credible use for all my GPS hardware.

I next thank Lincoln Turner, a long-time colleague and dedicated outdoor adventurer who, like me, is drawn to the slickrock canyons of southern Utah. His deep knowledge of traditional map and compass navigation techniques has made those chapters much richer than had I relied solely on my own experience.

I am particularly thankful for the assistance of Joe Mehaffey of gpsinformation.net. Widely recognized as one of the world's leading GPS authorities, his comments and suggestions on the technical aspects of GPS have significantly improved the accuracy of those sections of the book, though I will be quick to admit that any remaining errors are mine, not his.

My long-time distributor, Bob Lorentzen of Bored Feet Press, was particularly encouraging throughout the project. His knowledge and advice on the many technical aspects of publishing has been invaluable.

I'd also like to thank Art Reitsch, Doug Campbell, Larry Brenden, and Mike Alltucker, all photographers extraordinaire, whose conversations around lonely desert campfires have brightened many an evening in the wilderness. Their encouragement kept me writing and their photography keeps me inspired.

Finally, I'd like to recognize those people from the industry whose help has been invaluable: Steve Tatum of Lockheed Martin, Brendon Weaver of Brunton, Pete Brumbaugh of Garmin, Quinn Stone of Navicache.com, Ed McNierney of TopoZone.com, Bryan Roth of Groundspeak, Inc., Matt Heller and Cindy Beidel of National Geographic TOPO!, Inc., Ed Hall of Buxley's Geocaching Waypoint, and Jeffrey Bodzewski of Cobra. I also thank Chard Lowden of Sonoma Outfitters for his helpful comments on the manuscript.

Preface

YOU'D THINK THAT GPS MANUFACTURERS, after charging you a couple hundred dollars for one of their receivers, would want to make sure you really understood how to use it. After all, newspaper headlines blaring, "*Lost Hiker Found Dead Clutching GPS*," really don't do the industry any good. But GPS instruction manuals have long been notorious for seeming to be last minute afterthoughts. While they describe each of the receiver's dozens of functions in glossy detail, they never quite seem to explain how to use them to do anything useful, like actually navigate to a destination and return safely.

This neglect has led to the rise of a thriving cottage industry of aftermarket books, videos, and hands-on instructional classes. But even here, the consumer is likely to walk away confused. GPS is used in many different ways, from hiking in the woods to navigating aircraft to coordinating artillery strikes. In their attempt to wring every last dollar from the market, publishers often feel the need to cover in a single book all these different uses and more. It may look good on a book's dust jacket to proclaim it will teach you how to survey an archaeological dig or dock a supertanker, but if all you want to do is hike in the wilderness without getting lost, you'll probably find yourself overwhelmed.

The truth is that when it comes to wilderness navigation, using a GPS receiver is not all that complicated. That's true whether you're a hunter returning to your pickup after a day in the woods, a backpacker on a multi-day trek, or a geocacher searching for hidden treasures in a local park.

That's where this book comes in. You'll learn how to do the important things in a simple, easily-understandable way. You'll see how to keep from getting lost, how to navigate both simple and complex routes, and how to use your GPS receiver in combination with those two other venerable tools of the wilderness navigator, the map and compass. You won't be overwhelmed trying to understand the countless other GPS features you're unlikely to ever need. So don't worry if the instruction manual that came with your receiver forgot to show you how to navigate. You'll learn that here. Still, I can't explain why the manufacturers don't do a better job of covering this themselves. You'd think they'd at least be worried about potential lawsuits from customers.

Which brings me to the next important topic. As I've said, GPS is used in many different ways. Our subject is wilderness navigation. We'll see how to find your way in the outdoors but we won't cover such other uses as marine or aircraft navigation. If you really want to use GPS to do something dangerous like land an aircraft in a hailstorm or row solo across the Atlantic, you can start with this book but you'll need to follow up with expert instruction covering your specific needs.

There are dozens of different GPS receivers on the market today, and we can't cover everything about all of them. So we'll spend our time learning the *concepts* of GPS navigation, and we'll illustrate them with the kinds of receivers used in the outdoors. That way you'll be able to use what you learn regardless of what receiver you own today or which one you might buy next year. Don't throw away that instruction manual—you'll still need it. This book covers things your instruction manual should have explained but didn't. While we'll see plenty of examples using real GPS receivers, we won't repeat the exact button sequences for every receiver out there. Before you go charging off on some really difficult adventure like paddling up the Amazon or solo hiking to the South Pole, get plenty of practice on lesser challenges. Spend some time using your receiver in the yard, around the neighborhood, in nearby parks—places where if you make a mistake, you won't need a search-and-rescue team to retrieve you. In fact, my strong words of advice are that until you're completely comfortable with GPS and can routinely navigate without making mistakes, don't use your GPS receiver to take you anywhere you can't find your way back from without it.

Remember, a GPS receiver is a precision electronic instrument. While it's fairly rugged, it's not indestructible. Batteries can run down, it can get damaged from rough handling, or you can lose it off a hundred-foot cliff. Before you start out on any serious wilderness exploration, make sure you carry a map and compass and know how to use them. Although we won't cover everything you'll want to know about map and compass navigation, we'll give you enough information to get by in a pinch.

Terminology clarification

Technically speaking, the term "GPS" describes the entire global positioning system. What you hold in your hand is a "GPS receiver." Lots of people just call it a "GPS," but I'll try to avoid that in this book. A slang term to describe a GPS receiver that's gained popularity in the geocaching community is "GPSr." It remains to be seen how widely it will be adopted, so I won't use it here. If you want to understand the many other GPS-related terms, check the glossary at the back of the book.

Who should read this book

If you want to know how to use GPS for recreational adventures such as hiking, backpacking, hunting, fishing, river rafting, kayaking, mountain biking, snowshoeing, outdoor photography, or the fast-growing sport of geocaching, this book is for you. Our focus is on practical applications, not technical theory. You'll learn the things you need to know to be successful and safe, and to get the most enjoyment out of your investment. The theory we'll cover is limited to what you need to know to achieve success. If you really want to know the gory technical details of such things as satellite PRN sequences or dilution-of-precision errors, there are plenty of advanced textbooks and Internet websites out there.

You don't even need to own a GPS receiver. In fact, if you're thinking of making the investment but haven't yet done so, this book can help you make the best choice. And you might not even be all that interested in the subject yourself—spouses and significant others of GPS afficionados can also benefit. My wife, for instance, never showed much interest in GPS until one day she discovered the sport of geocaching. Now she's as likely to pull me along on an outdoor treasure hunt as I am to lead her into a backcountry exploration. Geocaching is a great sport for the whole family, combining elements of a treasure hunt, outdoor exercise, and navigation skills in a form that helps you quickly gain GPS experience.

GPS has rightfully been called the greatest advance in navigation since the invention of the compass. Even if you never expect to use it for anything more complicated than getting back to your car in a crowded parking lot, you'll find it useful. And once you know how to do that, it won't be long before you'll want to do more. Whatever your intended use, this book will help you get the most from your GPS receiver.

Stephen W. Hinch
Santa Rosa, California

Contents

PART 1:
Basic Navigation

Key Concepts in Part 1

- History of GPS
- How it works
- The four essential GPS skills
- Features of GPS receivers
- GPS limitations
- Waypoint basics
- Bearings: what they are and how to follow them
- The two most important GPS functions: MARK and GOTO
- All about compasses
- The difference between true and magnetic north

1
Basics of GPS

THE IDEA OF USING SATELLITES for navigation has been around since at least the late 1950s, when those few satellites in orbit were still the size of basketballs and neither the US nor the USSR had yet launched a man into space. Throughout the 1960s the Army, Navy, and Air Force all worked on various competing and incompatible systems. Government bureaucracy being what it is, it wasn't until 1973 that the Department of Defense decided it might be smart to combine all these efforts into a single program. Much to the Navy's chagrin, the Air Force got the nod to lead the development and operation of the new system, dubbed the *Navstar Global Positioning System.* Nowadays we just call it GPS. It's a way to quickly and easily find your position anywhere on earth.

Work progressed rapidly once the efforts were unified. The first prototype satellite was launched in 1978 and second-generation production versions beginning in 1989. The system was declared fully operational in 1995, after the last of the 24 second-generation satel-

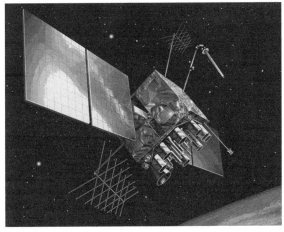

GPS satellite.
(Lockheed Martin
Space Systems Co.)

lites was deployed. The satellites have operational lives of between 3 and 10 years, so new ones are regularly launched to replace older ones before they go out of service.

GPS first gained worldwide fame in 1991 during Operation Desert Storm, the conflict that also brought us night-vision goggles and the Hummer. Television images of armored units being guided with pinpoint accuracy across a featureless Iraqi desert quickly captured the public's imagination. GPS was so widely used in Desert Storm that the military soon discovered they didn't have enough receivers to supply the troops. So they went out and bought over ten thousand consumer GPS units to make up the difference.

The fact there were even consumer GPS receivers to buy was not always a given. The military had imagined all sorts of ways GPS could be used against us by our enemies, and they were wary of letting the technology loose on the public. But the 1983 downing of Korean Air Flight 007 by the Soviet Union removed any doubt. This tragedy arose in part because the 747's flight crew made an error in navigation, and the xenophobic Russians shot them down. GPS, if it had been available, could have prevented that error. As a result, President Reagan issued a directive that GPS signals be made available free of charge to the entire world, and the commercial market has flourished ever since.

But the military was still wary. From the start, they had planned for a separate civilian version of the system whose accuracy could be degraded without affecting military operations. So in the early years they did just that, through a process known as Selective Availability, or SA. Civilian GPS was artificially degraded from its inherent 50-foot capability to something around 300 feet—the length of a football field.

For wilderness navigation, a 300-foot error isn't a catastrophe. If you can get within a few hundred feet of your destination you ought to be able to figure out the rest of the way on your own. But for aircraft and ships it could mean disaster. As you can imagine, SA caused considerable public outcry, particularly from commercial users. The Coast Guard and others even deployed their own enhancement to the system, called Differential GPS, that could completely eliminate the effects of SA to help ships safely navigate through harbors.

Finally, after numerous studies and considerable lobbying, President Clinton ordered that SA be permanently turned off beginning May 2, 2000. The improvement since that time has been remarkable. While the stated accuracy of civilian GPS is about 50 feet, most of the time you can find your position to 20 feet or less. The military, by the way, is still happy—they've figured out how to locally degrade civilian GPS accuracy wherever they're currently doing battle without affecting it in the rest of the world.

How it works

GPS works by the process of triangulation. It's the same theme you've seen in countless World War II movies. The heroic French resistance fighter hides in a farmhouse, using his clandestine radio transmitter to send vital military secrets to the Allies. All the while the Nazis are driving around in a big truck, listening in and trying to pinpoint his position. They invariably find him, but not until after he's sent the important information.

The Nazis used a technique called radio direction finding. With a radio receiver and an antenna that's very sensitive to the direction it's pointed, you can determine the direction a radio transmission is coming from. If you take readings from several different locations and plot them on a map, you'll find the transmitter located where all the lines intersect.

GPS is similar, with one significant difference. Instead of measuring the *direction* to each GPS satellite, your receiver measures the *time* it takes to receive each of their signals. Knowing the speed of light and the travel time of the signals, it can determine the distance to each satellite. It then has to figure out where each satellite is located in the sky. For this, it uses accurate information about satellite orbits stored in its internal memory. Once it knows the location of each satellite and how far away they each are, your receiver has everything it needs to calculate your position. The math is a little complicated, but that's something for your GPS receiver to worry about.

This only works if you know exactly when each satellite sent its signal and exactly when you received it, so accurate time is an essential part of the GPS system. All GPS satellites carry atomic clocks synchronized to three billionths of a second. Your handheld receiver, of course, doesn't include such a clock, but it doesn't need to. By tracking a fourth satellite it can lock onto the clocks in the satellites. Without that extra satellite, your receiver won't be nearly as accurate—in some cases it could be in error by over a mile. By the way, this ability to lock onto atomic clocks makes your GPS receiver the most accurate timepiece you can readily buy.

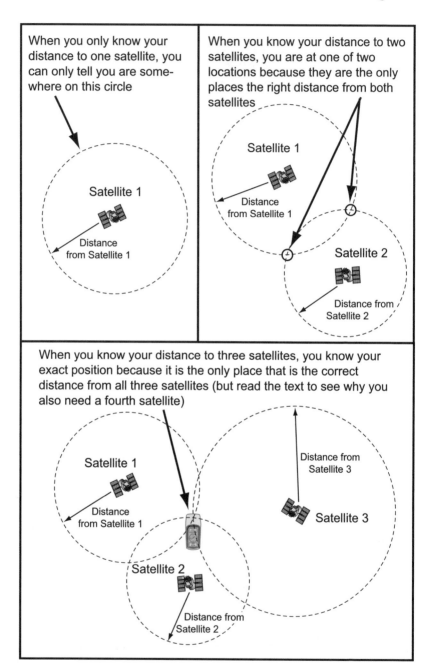

GPS works by a process of triangulation. To determine its position, a GPS receiver measures its current distance from at least three satellites. There is only one location the correct distance from all three satellites—your current position. A fourth satellite is needed to correct timing errors in the system.

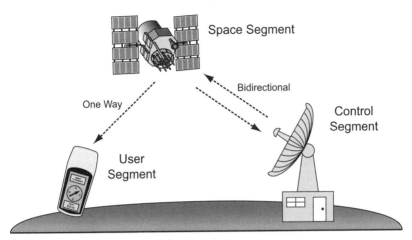

The three segments of the global positioning system.

There are three parts to the GPS system: the satellite segment, the user segment, and the control segment. Let's look at each of them in a little more detail.

Satellite segment. Satellites are the heart of the global positioning system. They broadcast the signals your receiver uses to determine your position. We'll learn more about the different types of signals in the next chapter. At least 24 satellites are in operation at all times, each orbiting the earth every 12 hours (11 hours and 58 minutes if you really want to be precise). Their orbits are designed so that theoretically, at least six and as many as twelve satellites are above the horizon virtually all the time regardless of where you are. "Theoretically" is the key word here—the satellite signals don't travel through mountains, buildings, people, or heavy tree cover, so unless you're on a flat plain or body of water, some signals will probably be blocked. Since your receiver must be locked onto at least four satellites to accurately determine its position, you may have to move around to get better reception. By the way, it's a little known fact that all GPS satellites actually perform a second duty. In addition to their GPS responsibilities, each also includes an X-ray detector that lets the government monitor nuclear explosions anywhere in the world.

User segment. Your handheld receiver makes up the user segment. There's a lot of power inside that little package. Not only does it contain a sensitive receiver capable of detecting signals less than a quadrillionth the power of a light bulb, it also includes a powerful computer that converts the raw data into such useful information as your position and speed. A GPS receiver doesn't include any kind of transmitter. GPS is a *passive* positioning system—you can determine your own position but there's no way for anyone else to track you.

Control segment. This is what keeps the whole system running smoothly. Satellites need to be kept in their proper orbits and their broadcast information kept up to date. The Air Force operates a series of five ground stations around the globe, typically at exotic tropical locations: Hawaii, Ascension Island, Diego Garcia, Kwajalein, and the decidedly non-tropical master station in Colorado Springs. You'll probably never think about the control segment, but without it the entire system would quickly fall into disrepair.

Today's basic 50-foot accuracy is sufficient for outdoor recreation but it's still marginal for certain commercial uses, primarily involving air or sea navigation. So you'll sometimes hear about two enhancements that have been made to further improve system accuracy. The first is the Coast Guard's Differential GPS, or DGPS. Although it was initially intended to guide ships on navigable waterways, their charter now extends to highway navigation as well. They operate over sixty ground stations throughout the country, each whose position has been accurately surveyed. Inside each station is a GPS receiver that compares the known location of the station with its position as measured by GPS. The difference is broadcast as a set of correction factors your receiver can use to improve its accuracy. Differential GPS allows you to reduce errors to just a few feet uncertainty.

To receive DGPS correction signals you need a separate, specialized receiver connected to your main GPS receiver. You also need to be in range of a ground station, so the technique has limited geographical coverage. The DGPS receiver, together with its antenna, are so large you need a backpack to carry them, so it's not really a practical solution for wilderness navigators.

Another enhancement that's getting a lot of publicity these days is the Wide Area Augmentation System, or WAAS. It uses several satellites in high-altitude geostationary orbits to measure system performance and broadcast correction factors that eliminate errors caused by current atmospheric conditions. Again, accuracies of a few feet

> ## The four essential GPS skills
> - Store your current location as a GPS waypoint
> - Return to a stored waypoint by following a bearing
> - Program waypoint latitudes and longitudes into your GPS
> - Navigate from one waypoint to the next in succession until you reach your final destination

are readily achievable. Many newer GPS units can receive WAAS corrections without any additional equipment, making it more attractive than DGPS. WAAS was primarily designed for aircraft navigation, but a lot of the publicity makes it sound like a panacea for all ills. But once again it's not all that useful for wilderness navigators. Only two satellites are visible from the United States, and they're both low in the southern sky. This isn't a problem for aircraft, but in many areas of the country the satellites aren't reliably visible from the ground. Another variant, LAAS, or Local Area Augmentation System, is even less useful. It's designed to guide aircraft on final approach and landing, so it only operates in the immediate vicinity of major airports.

Don't worry about using DGPS, WAAS, or LAAS in the outdoors. In fact, if you have a WAAS-enabled receiver you're usually better off disabling that feature and conserving battery power. I've never even needed WAAS accuracy to find hidden geocaches, probably the most exacting recreational use of GPS you're ever likely to do.

GPS in the wilderness: essential skills

In the simplest sense, a GPS receiver measures your exact position anywhere on earth, but navigation in the wilderness involves much more than knowing where you are. In fact, now is a good time to introduce what I call the *Cardinal Rule of GPS Navigation:*

It doesn't do you any good to know where you are if you don't know where you want to go.

The real contribution of GPS isn't showing you where you are, but showing how to get where you want to go.

The problem is complicated by the fact that GPS receivers report numerous other pieces of information besides your current position. How do you know what's important and what isn't?

First remember that all GPS receivers really only measure three things: your *position,* your *speed,* and the *current time.** All the other features—things like distance, bearing, map location, and even such vital details as sunrise and sunset or the best fishing times—are just calculations your receiver makes from those three measurements. That's why even the least expensive units work fine for outdoor navigators. They might not offer a lot of extras, but they all do the few things you really want.

So what are those few things? For outdoor navigation there are only four things you should really know how to do with your GPS receiver. If you can do these, you can successfully navigate in the wilderness. They are:

- Know how to store your current location in GPS memory. This is known as *marking a waypoint.*
- Know how to get back to that stored location from wherever you might be. You'll do this by the technique of *following a bearing.*
- Know how to program into your GPS receiver the coordinates of locations you want to go to. This is known as *entering a waypoint.*
- Know how to navigate from one stored waypoint to the next in succession until you get to your final destination. This is known as *following a route.*

It's as simple as that. If you know how to do those four things, you'll be able to get where you want to go and you'll be able to return safely. Most of the rest of this book shows you how to do them. We'll also discuss the important topic of what to do when your GPS receiver fails. And to keep all this knowledge from going to waste, we'll finish up with some fun things to do with GPS.

---

* *More expensive receivers sometimes include a true magnetic compass and barometric altimeter, but these are completely separate instruments that don't use GPS to make their measurements.*

GPS Accuracy

Just how accurate is the global positioning system? It's surprisingly difficult to get a good answer to that question. Some sources say a consumer GPS receiver is accurate to within 100 feet. Others report it as 50 feet. Manufacturers often give even better numbers, in the vicinity of 20 feet or less. What's the true story?

First, don't depend on your receiver to tell you. Although many receivers report something called *estimated position error or EPE*, it is not very accurate. This estimate is based only on satellite geometry and doesn't take into account the various other sources of error. Second, remember that until May 2, 2000, Selective Availability was the most significant source of error. Anything you read that was published before then is probably out of date.

The next thing to do is see what the Department of Defense says. After all, they operate the system so they ought to know its performance, right? But they aren't as much help as you'd wish. In a typically conservative fashion they don't actually specify total system accuracy, only the part within their direct control, which they call the *Signal-in-Space*, or *SIS*. This only defines the accuracy of the signals as they radiate from the satellites. It leaves out errors introduced as the signals propagate through the atmosphere.

Unfortunately, ever since the demise of Selective Availability, the atmosphere—especially the ionosphere—is the most significant source of GPS error. Just as the moon and sun look distorted as they drop low in the sky, signals from GPS satellites are bent as they travel through the atmosphere. They also experience delays that vary depending on the time of day, current solar activity, and moisture level in the air. GPS manufacturers use mathematical models to predict and compensate for these errors, but atmospheric conditions are never truly constant.

The DoD estimates the accuracy of civilian GPS to be better than 50 feet at least 95% of the time, anywhere in the world. This is what's called the *2drms* (twice the distance root-mean-square) accuracy. It is based on statistics. Don't worry about the math, just remember that the 2drms number means that over an entire day, a receiver's accuracy should be better than 50 feet at least 95% of the time.

Not all manufacturers specify their receivers this way. Some specify a simple rms value, which is half the 2drms number. It is a smaller number, but you will only see this accuracy two-thirds of the time. Still others report a *Circular Error Probable, or CEP*. This is an even smaller number but you will only be that close to your destination half the time. By specifying simple rms or CEP, manufacturers can make the numbers look better but the receiver may not be any more accurate. The 2drms accuracy is a conservative number. It's twice as large as simple rms and 2.4 times larger than CEP accuracy for the same receiver.

Another unpredictable effect is called multi-path error. Satellite signals are reflected by such things as tall buildings or canyon walls, and this can confuse your receiver as it tries to determine its distance from a satellite. Unfortunately there's not much a receiver manufacturer can do to eliminate this error. You have to move your receiver away from the offending object.

If the government only claims 50-foot 2drms accuracy, you might wonder how manufacturers can claim better performance. Two factors come into play. First, the 50-foot number is a very conservative estimate that applies anywhere in the world.

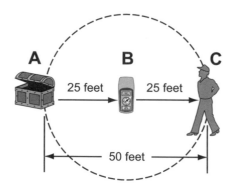

The error in returning to a previously marked waypoint is worse than the error in finding your absolute position, although you are unlikely to encounter this worst-case example.

You would probably only see such performance on rare occasions. Second, manufacturers continue to improve their software models of the ionospheric effect, so today's receivers are slightly more accurate than those produced a few years ago.

Civilian receivers operate on a single frequency, called L1, at 1575.42 MHz. Military receivers use both L1 and a second frequency, called L2, at 1227.6 MHz. This second frequency contains an encrypted code available only to the military that allows the receiver to completely eliminate the effect of the ionosphere.

Consumer receivers will get you to within about 25 feet of your intended destination most of the time. While manufacturers will undoubtedly continue to improve their software, you won't see much more improvement without the help of DGPS or WAAS. Beginning in 2005, the DoD is scheduled to begin launching a new series of satellites giving civilians access to a second satellite signal different from L1. When fully deployed, consumer receivers will be able to completely eliminate the ionospheric error, so you will get WAAS accuracy without the need for WAAS reception. But you'll need a new GPS receiver to take advantage of this improvement.

Finally, understand there is a difference between how accurately a receiver can determine its position and how accurately it will take you back to that position later. To understand why, refer to the diagram. Suppose you want to record the coordinates of Position A, where you have just placed a hidden treasure. Because your receiver can only determine your position to within about 25 feet, the coordinates it gives you might be those of Position B, 25 feet away from the true location. When you mark the position as Waypoint A, you are actually storing the coordinates of where your GPS receiver thinks it is—Position B—not where you actually are, Position A.

When you later want to find the treasure, you tell your receiver to go to Waypoint A. It will actually try to guide you to its stored location, Position B. But once again, because of system inaccuracies you can only get to within perhaps 25 feet of that location. Depending on your luck, you could end up right on the treasure or as far away as Position C, which is 25 feet away from position B and 50 feet away from your intended destination. In reality, you are unlikely to ever encounter this worst case example. A more realistic estimate takes the receiver's specified accuracy and multiplies it by factor of 1.4. This suggests you should routinely be able to return to within 35 feet of a previously stored location. But just remember that once in awhile, your error will fall outside this estimate.

2
GPS Receivers

Y OU CAN BUY A GPS RECEIVER to fit almost any budget, from a basic entry-level product to a deluxe model costing many hundreds of dollars. Not all of them are suitable for exploring the backcountry. In this chapter we'll learn what you need to know about GPS receivers for the outdoors—what features are essential, which are merely nice, and what to avoid. First, though, we'll need to learn a bit more about how they work.

Satellite signals

As you learned in Chapter 1, a GPS receiver works by measuring its distance from each of several satellites. Because it knows the exact location of each satellite, your receiver can calculate its position anywhere on earth. This is known as obtaining a *position fix*. But before it can do this, your receiver must obtain quite a bit of information from each satellite: its precise orbit, the time delay between when the satellite signal was sent and when it was received, and the exact GPS time.

Tools of the outdoor navigator: map, compass, and GPS receiver. These Garmin receivers span the range from entry-level (left) through intermediate (center) and full-featured mapping receivers.

Each satellite broadcasts several types of data. Once you see how this all works, you'll understand why your receiver sometimes gets a position fix right away and other times takes a lot longer.

Here's a brief description of the different types of data your receiver needs to calculate its position:

Almanac data. Although there are 24 satellites in the sky, their orbits are such that not all are simultaneously visible from any one location on earth. As few as six and at most twelve may currently be visible from your present location. It's hard enough for your receiver to detect signals that are actually there; it needs help so it doesn't waste time looking for satellites on the other side of the globe. Your receiver stores a table of information about satellite orbits, called *almanac data*, that it uses to predict which satellites should be visible. It's not very precise information, but it's good enough to tell which satellites should be above the horizon.

Your receiver gets its almanac data from the satellites themselves. Each satellite broadcasts the complete almanac for the entire array of 24 satellites, so you only need to be receiving one satellite to collect the information. Once your receiver has loaded a current almanac, the information stays valid for about six months. It's a good thing, too, because if you let the almanac get out of date by not using your receiver for an extended period, it takes at least 12½ minutes to download a new almanac. If you ever find yourself in this situation, turn your receiver on, set it somewhere it has a clear view of the sky, and go have dinner. When you return it should be finished downloading the new almanac. This is known as *initialization*.

If you have moved more than a few hundred miles from your last position or have not used your receiver in several months you may have to perform an initialization procedure. Mapping receivers like this Lowrance iFinder make this easier by allowing you to move a pointer to your approximate position on the map screen. (Courtesy of gpsinformation.net)

You may also have to initialize your receiver if you've moved more than a few hundred miles from your last position. If you're in San Francisco and the last time you used it was in London, your receiver will still think it is in London and look for satellites that aren't above the local horizon. After unsuccessfully searching for a few minutes it may ask you to input the state or country you're in, and perhaps what time it is, before it can find its position.

Ephemeris data. Almanac data is not accurate enough to determine your exact distance from a satellite. For this, your receiver needs very accurate satellite orbital information. Each satellite broadcasts information about its own orbit, called *ephemeris data*, which takes about 30 seconds to receive. Your receiver needs ephemeris data from least four satellites, so it can take as long as two minutes to download. Most receivers can speed the process by downloading from multiple satellites at once, reducing the total time to less than a minute. Ephemeris data stays valid for a few hours, so as long as you occasionally turn on your receiver during the day, you won't lose time waiting for this information to reload.

PRN code. This is the signal your receiver uses to measure the transmission time delay from each satellite. Civilian GPS uses a binary code that's 1023 bits long and takes 1 millisecond to transmit. (Military GPS uses a code that is 6 days long and much harder to jam!) PRN, in case you wondered, stands for "pseudo-random noise." It's a noise-like signal that is relatively easy to detect and fairly difficult to jam.

Your receiver tracks these signals on up to 12 satellites simultaneously. But that's not all. The job is made even more difficult because all 24 satellites broadcast this infomation on *exactly the same frequency*. To understand the challenge this presents, think of it this way. Suppose you've just settled down in front of your TV to watch a rerun of your favorite TV show, *Friends*. But your TV isn't quite working properly, so when you turn it on not only do you see *Friends*, there's also a ghost image of *Gilligan's Island* from the adjacent channel. Your job is to follow what's going on with Rachel and Ross while ignoring what's going on between the Professor and Maryanne.

Your GPS receiver has a similar task, but the analogy is that instead of ignoring *Gilligan's Island* it is enjoying both shows simultaneously.

In fact, it's not really happy unless it's watching at least four shows, and it can watch up to 12 shows at once without losing track of what any of the characters in any of the shows is doing! It's the ultimate in multitasking, the goal every good couch potato strives for—watching a dozen shows at once without ever having to use the remote control to switch between them!

Features of GPS receivers

Like everything electronic, GPS receiver technology is rapidly advancing. Size, weight, and power consumption drop every year. It's now possible to buy a GPS receiver built into your wristwatch, your mobile phone, or your handheld two-way radio. Who knows what you're likely to see in the next few years.

For wilderness navigation you don't really need a lot of receiver horsepower; you'll be more concerned with keeping down size and weight. Of course if you can afford it, you'll certainly want to consider a receiver with more features, but the minimum feature set you need includes the ability to do the following:

- Report your position in latitude and longitude
- Accept different map datums. In North America the absolute minimum includes the two formats known as WGS 84 and NAD 27
- Determine your speed and direction of travel
- Store the locations of numerous points of interest, called *way-points*
- Calculate the direction and distance from your current location to any stored waypoint and from one waypoint to another
- Plot a "breadcrumb" trail, or *track log*, of your path as you move around

We'll learn about waypoints and bearings in the next chapter. Latitude, longitude, and map datums are covered in Chapter 4. Track logs are described in Chapter 12.

GPS receivers for outdoor use come in three levels of complexity. *Entry-level receivers* are inexpensive units that provide all the basic features you need but not much

The Garmin Rino is a GPS receiver built into a 2-way radio.

more. *Intermediate receivers* have additional software features and usually include at least some sort of city database or mapping capability. *Full-featured mapping receivers* have advanced mapping capability that shows nearby towns, rivers, roads, and sometimes topographic features. More expensive versions include such additional features as a barometric altimeter or magnetic compass. Mapping receivers typically come with a built-in base map of major North American cities and highways. By purchasing additional software you can load more detailed street or topographic maps limited only by the receiver's available memory.

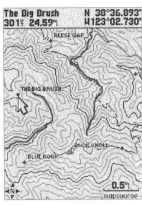

Mapping receivers such as this GPSMAP 76 can display detailed topographic maps.

Outdoor navigation doesn't require a high-end receiver. What you want as a minimum is one that is small and lightweight, has waterproof construction, and includes the minimum features listed above. If you're only going to use it for outdoor recreation and can't afford to spend a lot of money, a basic entry-level receiver will do fine. Ignore Internet reviews that disparage low-end products. Modern name-brand receivers work just fine, although there's always a chance you'll outgrow them and eventually long for more features. Extra gadgets like true barometric altimeters or magnetic compasses are fun toys if you can afford them, but hardly essential. By the way, that doesn't mean a magnetic compass isn't important—it is. It's just not necessary to have it built into your receiver. In fact, as I'll stress more than once, even if your receiver includes a built-in magnetic compass, my strong advice is that you still carry a separate compass. It's never smart to pin all your navigation hopes on the vagaries of a single battery-powered electronic instrument, no matter how much you paid for it!

If you also intend to use it for highway navigation you'll want a more expensive receiver with mapping capability. Here you'll have to make a tradeoff. Smaller, lighter units have smaller screens that are a little harder to see while driving. Larger units with bigger screens are great on the highway but cumbersome on a hike. In my opinion smaller is better, so I'll take what I get while driving. But you may make a different tradeoff. Just make sure you don't buy a unit dedi-

Compare the screen resolution of an entry-level eTrex (left) to that of the eTrex Vista (right). The Vista is a mapping receiver that needs a higher-resolution display. Despite their appearances, these compass displays are not a substitute for a magnetic compass.

cated only for highway use that doesn't have the waypoint and tracking features you'll need in the wilderness. The following paragraphs show you what to look for, starting with a discussion of key GPS features. For detailed information on current models suitable for outdoor navigation, refer to Chapter 13.

Display. Most receivers use black-and-white LCD displays. These don't consume a lot of power and are easily visible in the outdoors. Most allow you to activate a backlight so you can read the display in the dark. Inexpensive receivers don't need to show a lot of data and can get away with low-resolution displays. Mapping receivers need higher resolution. A few more expensive units have color displays, which can be an advantage in a mapping receiver that must portray a lot of information at once. In the past, color displays were more difficult to read in bright sunlight, but manufacturers continue to make improvements here.

Antenna. Your receiver will use one of two types of antennas, either a patch antenna or a quadrifilar helix antenna. Quadrifilar helix antennas are coils of wire beneath a plastic cover that typically extends beyond the main body of the receiver. Sometimes they are detachable, which can be useful in an automobile. In other units they are solidly attached but stick out from the top of the receiver.

Patch antennas look like small rectangular metal sandwiches. They're easy to build into the main receiver unit, so if yours doesn't have some sort of appendage sticking out of it, it probably uses a patch antenna. Either kind works well if you hold the unit properly. Units with a patch antenna, like the Garmin eTrex series, get best reception when held horizontally. Units with a quadrifilar helix antenna, like the Magellan Meridian series, typically should be held vertically. But this isn't always the case, so check your instruction manual for more information.

Some receivers have a connector that allows you to attach an external antenna. While not essential, this can be a useful feature. In a car, it allows you to mount the receiver on a dashboard bracket for easy viewing and still place the antenna where it has a good view of the sky. In the field, you can attach the antenna to your clothing and put the receiver in your pocket. This is great if you want

Garmin GPS 12XL with external antenna.

to record a continuous track of your journey, such as when you're mapping out the complete route of a new hiking or biking trail. Any receiver placed in your pocket will likely lose satellite reception, so without an external antenna you'll need to keep it out where it has a good view of the sky. Sadly, as receivers continue to shrink in size and cost, manufacturers more often see external antenna connectors as a needless extravagance.

Receiver. Inside the unit behind the antenna is the receiver system. All modern receivers are true 12-channel receivers—they can simultaneously track up to 12 satellites. Some older models had only one- or two-channel receivers. But they still needed to track four satellites to get a position fix, so they had to sequentially switch between the different satellites. It's the equivalent of a TV couch potato trying to watch four different shows by using his remote control to switch through them in quick succession. Like the couch potato, these older receivers missed some information, so they took a lot longer to get a position fix and were never quite as accurate as true 12-channel receivers. If you're thinking of buying a used receiver, make sure it has 12 *parallel*

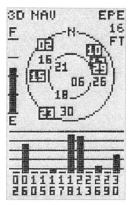

The satellite page shows the strength of each signal. This is the screen on the Garmin 12XL.

channels. Be careful, because some receivers were advertised as being able to "track up to 12 satellites" but could only track two satellites at a time.

Memory. This is most significant for mapping receivers. The receiver's built-in base map doesn't usually contain a lot of detail. It's typically limited to interstate highways, a few arterial roads, and major cities. If you want to do serious road navigation you'll need to buy a mapping software program from your receiver's manufacturer. Using a computer, you can then upload the additional information into your receiver. The amount of detail you can load will be limited by your receiver's memory. With 1 megabyte (abbreviated *MB*) you might be limited to the streets of a single city. With 24 megabytes you might be able to load a significant part of a state. Even with a 24-MB receiver, on a long cross-country trip you'll probably want to consider bringing a laptop computer to occasionally update your information. Some receivers accept external memory cards so you can easily swap data for different map regions. Others are limited to built-in memory and require that you download directly from a computer to modify the stored maps.

Mapping receivers from both Garmin and Magellan only accept maps from their own proprietary software programs. Each company offers various types of maps covering such things as metropolitan streets, highway points of interest, topographic features, or marine navigation aids and obstructions. Unfortunately, if you also use one of the excellent third-party topographic mapping software programs such as *Topo!* from National Geographic or *Terrain Navigator* from Maptech, you'll be disappointed to learn that while they'll let you upload waypoints and routes into your receiver, you won't be able to upload the maps themselves.

Computer Port. Many receivers let you transfer data between your receiver and personal computer. Most software programs have been designed for Windows PCs. Mac support is much harder to find. You can send information both ways—download stored waypoints and routes from your receiver to your PC or upload them from your PC to your receiver. You'll need two things to do this: some sort of software program to handle the exchange and a data cable that lets you connect your receiver to the PC.

You can get the software either from the receiver manufacturer or from third parties like National Geographic (http://maps.nation-algeographic.com/topo) or DeLorme (http://www.delorme.com). Remember that if you want to load actual maps into a mapping receiver (as opposed to just transferring waypoints, routes, and tracklogs), you're stuck with software from the receiver manufacturer.

At this writing, most handheld GPS receivers use serial ports for data transfer. There are a couple of problems with this approach. First, the transfer rate is excruciatingly slow. This is tolerable if you're only transferring waypoints and tracklogs, but to transfer 24 MB of map data takes over an hour. Second, serial ports are old technology and some newer PCs don't even come with one. It is possible to use a USB-to-serial converter, but manufacturers caution that not all such converters will work with their receivers. Garmin's GPSMAP 60C and 60CS are the first receivers designed for the outdoor market that provide the much-needed USB interface.

Power. As receivers continue to get smaller and lighter, their power requirements are also dropping. It wasn't long ago that the smallest receivers were powered by 4 AA cells. Now they use only 2 AA cells, and some even use AAA cells. A minor tradeoff is that battery life is usually shorter. Units with 2 cells typically run for about 12-15 hours. Older units could squeeze 24 hours or more from 4 cells. But the savings in size and weight more than make up for the difference. And if you're wondering how you'll get through a 3-day hike with a receiver that only runs for 12 hours, understand that you shouldn't need to leave it on all the time. Just turn it on for a few minutes whenever you need a position fix or an updated bearing and distance to your destination. With this approach you should be able to get through even a two-week journey without problem. And if you're concerned, you can always pack extra batteries.

It's a little different if you're using your receiver in a car. In this case you'll probably leave it turned on for extended periods, so you'll want to spend extra money on a cable that lets you plug it into your car's cigarette lighter. If this kind of use will be important, make sure to buy a receiver that can operate from external power.

Data Reporting and Analysis. Most GPS receivers designed for outdoor use can give you far more information than you're ever likely to need. The following list is primarily useful to weed out receivers that really aren't intended for wilderness navigation. All of these features

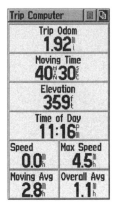

A typical GPS receiver can display a wide variety of data about your trip. The trip computer screen of the eTrex Vista allows you to customize what data is shown. Most of this information will only be accurate if you remember to clear memory before starting on your trip.

will be discussed more fully in later chapters. Here's what to look for:

- **Position format in latitude and longitude.** Most people will never need to use anything else, although inveterate backpackers occasionally swear by the UTM coordinate system. Any good unit will also have a dozen or more other formats that look good on the data sheet but you'll probably never use—the West Malayan RTO and the EOV Hungarian Grid are two that come to mind!
- **Map datum choices that include at least WGS 84 and NAD 27.** WGS 84 is the native datum of the GPS system, and NAD 27 is a North American datum used on many older topographic maps. We'll learn about these in Chapter 4. As with position format, most receivers provide dozens of other datums, including such all-time favorites as Liberia 1960 and Ascension Island 1958. Admittedly, a few of these will be important if you intend to do much international travel, but mostly they just clutter up the screen and make it harder to find those you really need.
- **Ability to mark and store waypoints.** This is one of the two most important features you'll use. You'll learn more about waypoints in the next chapter. Look for a receiver that can store at least 500 waypoints.
- **Easily accessible GOTO function.** This is the second of the two most important GPS features, as it tells you the distance and bearing to your destination. We'll cover this in Chapter 3. Once upon a time all self-respecting receivers had dedicated GOTO buttons, but nowadays some of the smaller ones have given this up—you'll have to search for it buried among the various screen displays.

- **North reference.** You should be able to at least select between true north and magnetic north, as we'll learn in the next chapter.

- **Compass display.** This is where you'll find the two most important pieces of data you'll normally need, the bearing and distance to your intended destination. Although it's not a substitute for a true magnetic compass, the compass pointer is still useful. When you're moving, it does a pretty good job of showing you the direction to your destination. When you're stopped, though, it's useless. For applications such a geocaching where you're not likely to get lost, you may be able to get by with this display in place of a magnetic compass. For any serious wilderness navigation though, you should carry a separate compass. Many receivers allow you to change this display from one that looks like a compass to one that looks like a highway. Stick with the compass display.

GPS receivers like this Lowrance iFinder typically offer 100 or more datum choices. (Courtesy gpsinformation.net)

- **Route capability.** This is a useful tool to guide you on a multi-part hike. It's like an enhanced GOTO function. You specify the way-points you want to go to and the sequence you want to reach them; the route function automates the process of going to each of them in succession. You could, of course, do the same thing manually using the GOTO function, but you're less likely to make a mistake if you've entered the information as a route.

Any receiver that offers all of the above features will probably offer many others. Some are useful, but most are just niceties. Sunrise, sunset, time of day, and trip odometer, for example, could provide useful information. Glide ratio, velocity made good, and estimated time of arrival are really designed for aircraft or marine navigation and won't have much use in the outdoors.

Limitations of GPS

GPS is so powerful it's easy to forget it also has limitations. These are especially likely to show up in wilderness navigation so it's important

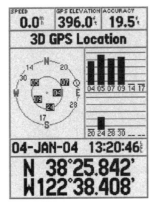 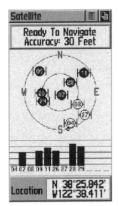

Be sure you know how to tell your receiver is operating in 3D mode. The Garmin GPSMAP 76S (left) explicitly indicates its state. On the eTrex Vista (right) you must observe the satellite strength indicators to confirm at least 4 satellites are being tracked.

you understand and know how to deal with them.

Satellite visibility. Since it depends on satellites to operate, your receiver needs a clear view of the sky. As we've seen, it doesn't need to see the whole sky, but at least enough to lock onto four different satellites. So if you're in a narrow canyon or you're surrounded by tall buildings, your receiver probably won't work. Nor will it work indoors. And it might not work under heavy tree cover because the water in tree leaves blocks the satellite signals. In the forest, your receiver will actually work better in the fall and winter when the leaves have fallen from the trees. By the way, clouds, rain, and snow won't significantly affect your reception. A solid film of water blocks the signals but water vapor or isolated droplets don't. That's also why you can't use a GPS receiver under water.

This is one area where a larger receiver might work better because it will probably have a more sensitive antenna. But even the best receiver won't work in confined areas. The satellite page will help you see how good your reception is. Check it occasionally. With practice, you'll get good at predicting when you're about to lose coverage.

Needs at least four satellites. For best accuracy, your receiver must be locked onto at least four satellites. This is called the *3D operating mode* because it accurately finds your position in all three dimensions. But sometimes terrain or tree cover will block some signals and your receiver won't lock onto four satellites. If it can lock onto three satellites it will operate in what's known as 2D mode. It will still calculate a position but it probably won't be very accurate. In 2D mode your receiver has to compensate for the missing satellite. It does this by assuming your elevation. The only elevation it knows is the last one it measured, so that's what it uses. But if you've changed your position since then, your elevation could have changed by hundreds or thousands of feet and the calculated position can be in error by a mile or more. If you know your current elevation you can somewhat improve accuracy by manually entering it into your receiver. But in general, 2D navigation is nearly useless and even dangerous for wilderness navigation, so never depend on it.

If 2D mode is so useless, why do manufacturers provide it? Well, it does work on the ocean, where the elevation is constant. But on the ocean you almost always have a clear view all the way to the horizon, so it's easy to lock onto four satellites. 2D mode is a holdover from the early days of GPS before all 24 satellites were deployed. There's little need for it today.

Manufacturers don't do a very good job of explaining this limitation. Instruction manuals often refer to the fact that "elevation is not being computed," but they don't explain the impact on accuracy. Some newer units don't even explicitly tell you whether they're operating in 2D or 3D mode. You have to figure it out for yourself by looking at the satellite page to see how many satellites are being tracked. Make sure you know how to tell your receiver is operating in 3D mode before you rely on its data.

Inaccurate elevation. GPS was designed to find your position anywhere on earth but it was not designed to accurately measure your elevation. Most GPS receivers will give you an elevation readout, but you can't depend on it. Its accuracy depends on the geometry of the satellites in the sky. When they are well spread out it can be reasonably accurate, but when they are closely grouped it can be in error by a thousand feet or more. If you really want accurate elevations you'll need to use a calibrated barometric altimeter.

Not a compass. Remember that a GPS receiver is not a compass. This is confusing to many people because every receiver has a screen that looks like a compass display. But it's not. It can only tell you what direction you're moving, not what direction it's pointed. So it is really a *heading indicator*, not a true compass. Wilderness navigation, even using GPS, depends on you accurately knowing direction, so you should always carry a separate magnetic compass.

Today, some receivers include a separate built-in magnetic compass. Known as an electronic fluxgate compass, it is accurate to within about 5°. But when turned on, it rapidly uses up batteries. And a receiver with a built-in magnetic compass can cost over $100 more than a similar one without it. You can get a quality magnetic compass for under $30. If you have a unit with a built-in compass, go ahead and use it, but still carry a separate compass. That way if your receiver gets damaged or its batteries fail, you're not completely helpless.

3
Navigation using Waypoints and Bearings

THE SIMPLEST THING YOU CAN DO with your GPS receiver is use it to find your way back to a location you've been to before—a favorite campsite, fishing spot, or even your car in the mall parking lot, for example. I call this "basic navigation" because you can use it without knowing anything about such things as latitude, longitude, position formats, or map datums. You just need to know how to store your current location as a GPS *waypoint* and how to return to it using your receiver's GOTO function. You'll also need to know how to navigate by *following a bearing*. So this chapter covers waypoints, bearings, and your receiver's GOTO function.

Consider an example. Suppose you intend to spend the afternoon exploring unfamiliar territory. Maybe you're a hunter going where the game takes you or a photographer looking for that great shot. Either way, you don't have a planned itinerary and might not follow established trails. You need to make sure you can get back to the trailhead before dark. So here's what to do: store the location of the trailhead as a GPS waypoint before you start out. Then when you're ready to return, let your receiver show you how to get back to it. If you know how to follow a bearing, you should have little trouble getting back. Let's explore the process in more detail, starting with a better understanding of waypoints.

Waypoints

Waypoints (sometimes called *landmarks*) are one of the most basic GPS concepts. What is a waypoint? Think of it as something like a street address. Suppose you live at 123 Center Street, Anytown, USA. Your address is simply a way to describe exactly where you live. It's how the Post Office knows where to deliver your mail, how the pizza parlor knows where to deliver that delicious dinner you ordered. Waypoints are the GPS equivalents of street addresses, but of course they aren't just limited to streets. The Global Positioning System uses a mathematical model of the entire earth to describe the coordinates of any point on it. Most often, this will be in the form of latitude and longitude, but your GPS receiver can use many other formats as well. In fact, regardless of what format you specify, your receiver always stores the information its own internal format referenced to the center of the earth. It applies complicated mathematical formulas to convert this internal format into something more useful to humans, like latitude and longitude or UTM coordinates.

Using waypoints it's possible to do things like record the position of a tree in your front yard separately from another tree in your backyard. But remember GPS accuracy is only about 25 feet, so don't depend on it to determine positions better than that. You can't use your consumer GPS receiver to accurately survey your property lines, for example, although it is possible to do so with certain very expensive commercial units and additional computer software.

A typical consumer GPS receiver can store 500 or more locations in its waypoint database. You can enter them in several ways. The simplest way, though not always the easiest, is to go to the desired location and push the buttons that tell your receiver to store your current location in memory. That's what we'll cover in this chapter. In Chapter 5 we'll see how to enter the latitude and longitude of a location without actually having to go there. And in Chapter 8 we'll see how to use a computer and mapping software to upload waypoints without having to arduously key in the numbers.

Once you've stored a waypoint, you can go wherever you want and your GPS receiver can always show you how far away and what direction that waypoint is from your current position. Then it's a simple matter of heading in the right direction until you get back to it. But to do this, you need to know a bit about direction-finding in the wilderness.

Directions and bearings

We are all familiar with how to describe directions in terms of the four cardinal points of the compass—north, south, east, and west. Intermediate directions include northeast, southeast, southwest, and northwest. Some GPS receivers even let you display bearings in this format. But it's not very precise.

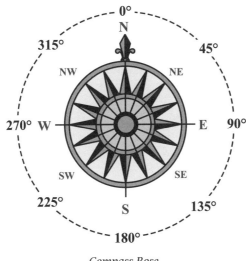

Compass Rose

A better way is based on the Greek system of dividing the full circle into 360°. North is defined as the reference direction at 0°. Going clockwise around the circle, east is at 90°, south at 180°, and west at 270°.

With this approach, you can describe a direction very accurately. A mountain in the distance that's directly east of you is said to be at a bearing of 90°. Another peak that's directly southwest is at a bearing of 225°. With care, using a good magnetic compass you can measure the bearing to a distant object to an accuracy of about 2 degrees. We'll learn how to do that later in the chapter.

In GPS terminology, the term *bearing** is used to describe the direction between your current position and your desired destination. In contrast, the term *heading* describes the direction you are actually traveling. If you're moving directly toward your destination then your heading and your bearing are the same. If not, they will be different. Often this will be unavoidable, as when you're navigating around an obstacle such as a mountain. You can set up your GPS receiver to display either value on its screen (see the figure on Page 47). Just make sure you understand the difference between the two terms, and that

---

* *Purists call this an* azimuth, *but the term* bearing *has become dominant in the GPS world.*

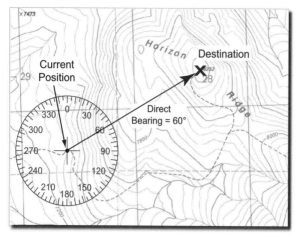

You can use a map to read the bearing from your current position to your destination. Draw a straight line between the two points and center a protractor over your current position with 0° oriented due north. Read the bearing where the line intersects the edge of the protractor.

you use bearing, not heading, to guide you to your destination.

When set to display numeric bearings, your GPS receiver can give you a bearing readout to 1-degree resolution. This is more than sufficient for outdoor navigation, where you'll rarely be able to follow a bearing to an accuracy of better than 5° anyway.

Remember that the bearing to an object is a relative, not an absolute number—it depends on where you are. If you're in San Francisco, for example, the bearing to Denver is about due east, or 90°. But if you're in Washington D.C., it is about due west, or 270°. So the bearing between you and a target object changes as you move around. Someone standing in a different spot will measure a different bearing to the same object. If the two of you are close together and the object is far away, the difference won't be much, but it's always something to keep in mind.

Once you understand the concept of bearings, you can use a map and protractor to find the bearing from your present position to any destination. Here's how. Using a ruler, draw a straight line on the map connecting your current position with your destination. Now take a protractor (those circular plastic things with numbers on them you haven't used since grade school) and center it over your current position. Orient it so that 0° points straight north. The bearing to your destination is where the line you drew intersects the edge of the protractor. Check the illustration to see how this works. Once you understand it, you're ready to learn how to navigate.

Simple navigation

Waypoints and bearings are fundamental to the concept of GPS navigation. To see why, let's go back to our example. Recall that you plan to spend the afternoon exploring unfamiliar territory and want to make sure you can get back to the trailhead before dark. So you need to store the location of the trailhead as a GPS waypoint. When you're standing at the trailhead this turns out to be pretty easy. You don't need to know anything about latitude or longitude. Just turn on your receiver, wait for it to find its position, then push the buttons to store that location in memory. This is known as *marking* a waypoint. Every receiver does this a little differently. Some have a dedicated MARK button; push it and it brings up the waypoint screen. Here you can do things like give the waypoint a name or assign it a symbol before you store it. Other receivers don't have a dedicated button—you must select the MARK feature located on one of the menu pages. Such receivers usually have a shortcut way to mark a waypoint, such as by holding down the ENTER key for a couple of seconds. You'll need to read your instruction manual for specific details.

By default, your receiver will identify the waypoint by assigning it a number, but this really isn't very useful. After a day of hiking, how likely are you to remember you car is at waypoint number 763? So you should give it a better name. Many receivers limit you to 6 alphanumeric characters, although some newer units allow more. Again, check your manual to see how to enter waypoint names for your unit.

Regardless of what receiver you own, entering waypoint names is usually a cumbersome process involving lots of button pushing. You'll need quite a bit of practice before you feel comfortable doing

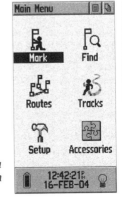 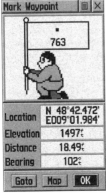

On the Garmin eTrex Vista, you access the MARK WAYPOINT screen from the MAIN MENU. You can also reach it by holding down the Click Stick for two seconds.

it. But it's important, so make sure you get that practice. In Chapter 8 you'll see how to use a computer to make the job easier.

There are a couple of things to remember when storing waypoints. First, make sure your receiver is operating in 3D mode, not 2D mode. Many receivers have an explicit 2D-3D indicator, but some newer receivers don't. In that case you might need to check the satellite page to verify it is tracking at least four satellites. Or check the value your receiver reports for its estimated position error (sometimes called EPE). If it's in the neighborhood of 20-30 feet or less, you're OK.

One more caution. Don't use the same name as a waypoint already stored in memory. Most receivers won't erase the existing waypoint but they don't always make it obvious they haven't stored the new one. This is most often a problem if you use the same name repeatedly, such as "CAR" to indicate the location of your car. So first check the list of existing waypoints and delete any previous waypoint with the same name. Some Garmin receivers have a nifty feature called REPOSITION HERE. You just call up an existing waypoint and with one touch you can reposition that waypoint to your current location.

Once you've stored the location of the trailhead, you are ready to go out and explore. So turn off your receiver and put it in your pocket. There's no reason to keep it turned on all the time unless you really want to record a complete track log of your journey as described in Chapter 12. Remember that leaving it on quickly uses up your batteries, and you probably won't get very good reception anyway if it's packed away in a pocket or backpack.

GOTO function

After a few hours of exploration, you're ready to return to the trailhead. Now it's time to turn on your receiver and use another important GPS feature, the GOTO function. With this feature, you tell your receiver what waypoint you want to go to and it automatically calculates the bearing and distance to it. Then you just follow the indicated bearing until you reach the car. We'll describe that process in a moment.

Again, you need to read your instruction manual to learn how to use your receiver's GOTO function. Some receivers have a dedicated GOTO button. You just push the button and select which waypoint you want to go to. With others, you first have to select the desired waypoint from the waypoint database, then select GOTO from a list of options.

The GOTO function is an essential feature. Know how to use it. The Garmin 12 XL (left) has a dedicated GOTO button. On the eTrex (right) it is a selection on the WAYPOINT screen.

Receivers often give you several ways to display the waypoint list. Typical choices include alphabetically, nearest, and favorites. Mapping receivers usually also give you other choices, including such things as cities and points of interest.

Once you've initiated the GOTO function, you should see the bearing and distance to the selected waypoint, although you might have to scroll through various pages to find the information. Usually, it will at least show up on the compass page, although with some receivers you have to make sure you have configured the display to show bearing rather than some dubious piece of information like Glide Ratio or Estimated Time Enroute. Once again, check your unit's instruction manual.

OK, that's great. You now know the bearing and distance to your

The compass page shows you the bearing and distance to a selected waypoint. This eTrex Vista can also be configured to show such other information as your current heading.

The Brunton Pocket Transit is an outstanding professional tool but may be more than necessary for the casual hiker. (Brunton)

destination. But how do you know which direction to hike? For that, you need to know how to use a compass to find and follow a bearing.

Magnetic compasses

While you can often use your GPS receiver's compass page to follow a bearing in the field, you really should understand how to use a magnetic compass. As I've already said, for any serious navigation you absolutely must carry a separate compass. So let's take a few minutes to understand compasses and how to use them.

Compasses come in many flavors, from dime-store novelties to precision instruments costing many hundreds of dollars. Geologists and foresters swear by the Brunton Pocket Transit, a survey-grade, all-brass compass that not only finds direction but also can be used to measure angles, height, and slope. It works great in the outdoors, but it's heavy, inconvenient, and expensive. You can get by with something much simpler and less expensive.

The Brunton is an example of a sighting compass, a class that also includes various military-type instruments. They are designed to read bearings to a precision of a degree or less, which can come in handy if you're trying to direct an air strike onto an enemy stronghold while avoiding our troops nearby. But it's overkill for wilderness navigators who usually aren't able to follow a bearing to better than 5° anyway.

The best choice for recreational outdoor use is the type called the *baseplate compass*. (You'll sometimes hear it described as an *orien-*

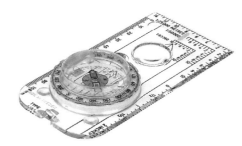

The baseplate compass is the best choice for general outdoor use. (Brunton)

teering compass.) Conveniently, you can get a good baseplate compass for around $20, and even the top-of-the-line units rarely cost more than $50. Popular manufacturers include Brunton, Silva, and Suunto.

Baseplate compasses

If wilderness navigation only consisted of knowing which way was north, then just about any compass would do. But in reality, navigation involves two very important steps. First you must determine the bearing from your present location to your destination. Then you have to decide what direction that is in real life. The advantage of a baseplate compass is it can help you in each of these situations. And it will also help on those occasions in the field when you want to read

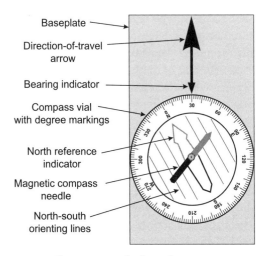

Baseplate

Direction-of-travel arrow

Bearing indicator

Compass vial with degree markings

North reference indicator

Magnetic compass needle

North-south orienting lines

Components of a baseplate compass.

A sighting mirror makes it easier to take accurate bearings in the field. An added benefit is that when the cover is opened all the way, it becomes a long straightedge for measuring bearings on a map. (Brunton)

the bearing from your current position to an object like a mountain or radio tower in the distance.

Study a baseplate compass and you'll see it has three parts: the baseplate, a compass vial, and a magnetic needle. First let's look at the baseplate. The most important thing you'll see on it is what's called a *direction-of-travel arrow*. On most compasses the arrow is printed along the center of the baseplate pointing away from the vial, but sometimes the end of the compass itself is shaped like an arrow. The opposite end of the arrow butts up against the compass vial at what is called a *bearing indicator*. This is what you use to find the direction to your destination. The baseplate also has at least one straight edge you can use to read bearings on a map.

The circular compass vial containing the magnetic compass needle is mounted to the baseplate. The vial is filled with liquid and has degree markings from 0 to 360 on its perimeter. The liquid damps the motion of the needle so it quickly stabilizes its position. (Compare this to cheap compasses where the needle gyrates wildly at the slightest motion, and you'll appreciate the improvement.) The vial is designed so you can rotate it by hand, but with enough friction so that once positioned, it stays put. Look through the vial to its bottom and you'll see what looks like the outline of a compass needle pointing to the 0 degree indicator on the perimeter of the vial. This is the *north reference indicator*. We'll see how to use it in a minute.

Some compasses include a sighting mirror. This makes it easier to take accurate bearings in the field because when you tilt the mirror at about a 45 degree angle and hold the compass at eye level, you can see the compass vial at the same time you are looking at the object whose bearing you want. It's nice, but it's not an essential feature.

Finding a bearing in the field

Let's get back to our example. You've been out in the wilderness for the afternoon and now you are ready to go back to the trailhead. You've turned on your GPS receiver and told it to go to the trailhead waypoint, which you've named START. Suppose your receiver says it's 1.5 miles away at a bearing of 135°. That's great, but you still need to know what direction that is in real life.

Here's how to use a baseplate compass to find out. Rotate the compass vial so that 135° is aligned with your bearing indicator. Then hold the compass at waist level so its direction-of-travel arrow is pointing directly away from you. Now your job is to orient the compass so that 0° on the vial is pointing directly north, because when that happens, you know your direction-of-travel arrow is pointing to a bearing of 135°. That's easy enough to do, because the magnetic needle shows you where north is. Just rotate your entire body until the compass needle is boxed inside the north reference indicator on the base of the vial. Make sure you get the correct end of the needle lined up with the correct end of the north reference indicator.

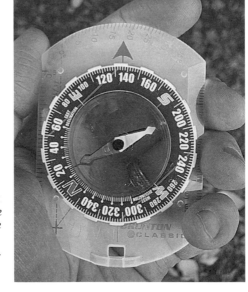

To find a bearing in the field, set the compass vial so the desired bearing aligns with the bearing indicator. Then rotate your entire body to box the magnetic needle inside the north reference indicator. The direction-of-travel arrow now points in the desired direction. Note this compass is set for 16° East declination.

Otherwise you'll head exactly opposite of your intended direction. Usually this means lining up the red end of the arrow with the red end of the indicator. Check out the illustration to get a better idea of the process. Once you've got the needle aligned inside the indicator, the direction-of-travel arrow points in the direction of 135°. Head in that direction for a mile and a half and you'll be at your car.

For those of you cringing and thinking to yourself "what about magnetic declination?" relax. We'll cover that question shortly.

One word of caution when using a magnetic compass. Because it's magnetic, it can be affected by nearby metal objects. Vehicles, metal signposts, and belt buckles are common offenders. Even the batteries in your GPS receiver can have an effect. Take off your backpack and stay away from iron or steel objects when taking a compass reading.

Common-sense navigation: following a bearing

Your GPS receiver can only show you the straight-line direction to your destination. It can't show you how to navigate around obstacles such as mountains, rivers, or forests. You'll rarely be able to walk a straight line in the wilderness, although something about GPS always seems to make people want to try. I can't tell you how many times I've watched otherwise sensible people, eyes glued to their receiver, go tramping through dense underbrush, poison oak, and hazardous terrain because "that's the direction my GPS told me to go." Not only is this potentially dangerous, it's a good way to harm a delicate natural environment. Ninety percent of the time you'll be able to get to your destination primarily by following established trails. Most of the rest of the time a little reconnaissance or advance planning will show you the most sensible route.

The best way to navigate with GPS is to do it the same way you would in the more traditional map and compass approach. Use your receiver to find the distance and bearing to your destination, then use your compass to see what direction that is. Look in that direction and pick a distant object like a tree, mountain peak, or telephone pole you can use as a reference point. Then *turn off your receiver and put it away.* Use your eyes and brain to find the best route to get to that object. Go *around* obstacles, not over the top of them. If you lose sight of your goal, pull out your receiver to get an updated bearing, then put it away. When you reach your first reference object, use your receiver to find the new bearing to your destination. Then pick out a new object in the distance and repeat the process. Keep it up until

When following a bearing, look for a feature such as a distant mountain peak in the desired direction. Then put away your GPS receiver and keep the feature in sight as you hike. Take the most logical route toward it rather than blindly following a straight line across difficult terrain. Use your GPS receiver to update the bearing to your destination occasionally, and select a new feature in the distance when necessary.

your get to your goal.

One of the most common mistakes made by novices is thinking the bearing they measured at the start of the hike is the same one they should use for the entire hike. They don't realize that unless you are moving directly toward your destination the bearing to it will change as you move. The great thing about GPS, though, is that's not a problem. Just remember to occasionally turn on your receiver and get a current update of the bearing and distance to your destination, then adjust your heading accordingly.

True vs. magnetic north

All this would be simple if a magnetic compass always pointed to the north pole, or *true north*. But for various complicated magnetohydro-dynamic reasons the earth's magnetic field isn't exactly aligned with its axis of rotation. This means a magnetic compass doesn't point to the true north pole but rather to a location in northern Canada called *magnetic north*. So when given a bearing, you need to know whether it is referenced to true north or magnetic north. In the US, if you are in the Midwest it doesn't much matter because the two are nearly the same. The *agonic line*, or line of zero declination, runs from northern Minnesota to the Florida panhandle. But as you move toward either coast, the more difference you'll see. As you move west, your compass points too far east. As you move east, it points too far west. The difference in direction between true north and magnetic north is called *magnetic declination* (called *magnetic variation* by mariners). It is measured in degrees, and you must specify whether it is east or west. East declination occurs whenever the magnetic needle points too far east; west declination when it points too far west. In the continental United States, declination ranges from about 20° east to 20° west. In Los Angeles, it's about 14° east. In New York City, it's about 13° west. In Alaska it's even worse, exceeding 35° in some areas.

What does this mean? Let's say you're near San Francisco, with a declination of about 15° east. If your GPS receiver is set to give you a bearing referenced to true north ("true bearing") but your compass is set to magnetic north ("magnetic bearing"), you will think you're going in the right direction when you are really headed 15° too far east. Walk only four miles in this direction and you'll have deviated a full mile from your intended path.

The same problem occurs when you read a bearing from a map. Most maps are designed so that true north is at the top of the page.

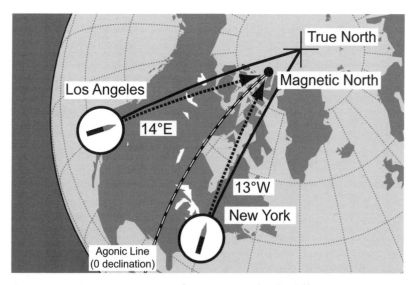

A compass points to magnetic north, not true north. The difference between the two directions is called magnetic declination.

A good compass allows you to compensate for magnetic declination. On the left, the compass is set for zero declination. On the right, it is set for 15° East declination. Notice how the north reference indicator no longer points to 0°. On this Suunto compass you set declination from the underside of the compass by turning the adjustment screw visible in the upper left portion of the black ring.

If you measure a bearing from a map and then use a magnetic compass to guide you in the wilderness, you'll have to compensate for declination.

Most books at this point admonish you to memorize the mathematics that convert from true to magnetic bearings and back, with dubious mnemonics like "east is least, west is best." But I'm not going to do that here. If you really want to know how to do the math, read the sidebar. My advice is to avoid the whole issue by buying a compass with adjustable declination and setting it to the local declination. That way you don't have to worry about the difference.

Here's how it works. Remember that the north reference indicator on a compass vial normally points to the 0° marking on its perimeter. This means that when you center the magnetic needle inside the indicator, your compass is oriented so that 0° points to *magnetic* north. But you'd really like 0° to point to true north. So some compasses allow you to adjust the north reference indicator to compensate for declination. Such a compass has a separate declination scale calibrated in degrees east and west, and it allows you to change where the north reference indicator points. For example, to set your compass for 15° east declination, adjust the north reference indicator so it is pointing to 15E on the declination scale. Conversely, if you want to set it for 15° west declination, adjust the indicator to 15W on the declination scale. Some compasses provide a little screwdriver on the lanyard you can use to make the adjustment. With others, you do it by hand without any tools. Either way, once it's set you don't have to worry about doing mental math after an exhausting ten-hour hike. There's still the little matter of knowing the declination for your location. One way to find out is to check a recent topo map of the area. Magnetic declination is almost always indicated on a topo map, either graphically or in text. Or you can find it from the NOAA magnetic declination website, http://www.ngdc.noaa.gov/cgi-bin/seg/gmag/ declination1.pl, by entering the Zip code or latitude and longitude of the desired location. You can even look it up on your GPS receiver. Go to the SETUP (sometimes called SYSTEM) page and select the feature called "North Reference." Normally, it should be set to TRUE north. But if you change the setting to MAGNETIC (sometimes called AUTO), it will show the declination of your current position to the nearest degree. Make sure you set it back to TRUE north when you are finished!

In the continental US, magnetic declination changes only gradually as you change your position. You should easily be able to move a hundred miles or more before it's enough different to worry about resetting your compass.

If you're only ever going to follow GPS bearings and never measure them from a map, you have one other alternative. You can leave your receiver set to MAGNETIC north. By setting your GPS receiver to display magnetic bearings you can use a simple compass and not have to worry about declination adjustments. But you'll still need to correct for declination if you ever use your compass to read bearings from a map.

Magnetic declination varies over time. Over the last hundred years the magnetic pole has moved over seven hundred miles north. In some areas this has caused a change of over a degree of declination every 10 years. So check the publication date of any map you use. If

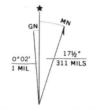

Declination is almost always shown on a topographic map. On USGS maps, the star indicates true north, MN indicates magnetic north, and GN indicates grid north, used only in the UTM system. Don't depend on the drawn angle to accurately represent the true declination.

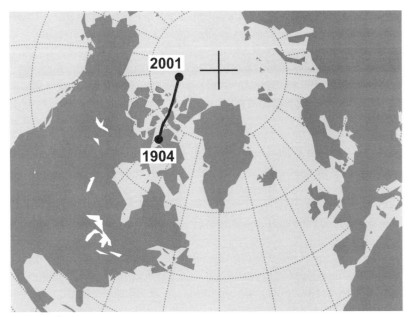

The magnetic north pole has moved over 700 miles northwest in the last hundred years.

it's over 10 years old its declination information could well be out of date. The information on the NOAA website is always current.

Don't forget to check the north reference setting in your receiver. There are usually several choices. TRUE bearings are referenced to true north. MAGNETIC (sometimes called AUTO) bearings are referenced to magnetic north. Your receiver uses a table stored in memory to compute magnetic declination, so after many years, it will get out of date. A third choice labeled USER allows you to manually set declination. Other choices can include such little-used favorites as GRID, MILITARY TRUE, or MILITARY MAGNETIC. As a civilian wilderness navigator you will probably never need to worry about these.

Summary of simple navigation

Now let's summarize the process of storing your present location and using your GPS receiver to return to it later.

Setup:

1. Before you begin, check the north reference setting on your receiver. Select *True North* when using a magnetic compass with

adjustable declination that's set for your local declination.
Select *Magnetic North* if your compass doesn't have adjustable
declination.

2. If using a compass with adjustable declination, set it to your local
   declination. Check a recent topo map or the NOAA website if you
   don't know the local declination.

At the trailhead:

1. Turn on your GPS receiver and wait for it to acquire a position fix.
   Confirm it is operating in 3D mode, not 2D mode.
2. Decide on to an easily-remembered waypoint name such as
   "TRAIL" for a trailhead or "CAR" for you car. Call up your receiver's waypoint list and delete any existing waypoint with the same
   name.
3. To store your present location, select the MARK function. Do this
   by pressing the MARK button (if your receiver has one), selecting
   MARK from the appropriate menu page, or using the MARK shortcut (if your receiver has one).
4. When the MARK WAYPOINT page is displayed, change the waypoint name from the default number to the name you have chosen.
5. Select the command to store the waypoint. On Garmin receivers
   this is usually the choice labeled "OK." On Magellan receivers it is
   labeled "SAVE."
6. Go to the waypoint database and confirm your waypoint has been
   stored.

When ready to return:

1. Turn on your receiver and wait for it to acquire a position fix.
2. Select the GOTO function. Some receivers have a dedicated GOTO
   button. Others require that you select a specific waypoint from the
   database, then select the choice labeled GOTO.
3. On the receiver's compass page, note the distance and bearing to
   your destination.

Navigating to your destination:

1. Set your compass so the GPS bearing to your destination is aligned
   with the direction-of-travel indicator.
2. Hold the compass in front of you at waist level with the direction-
   of-travel arrow pointing directly away from you. Rotate your entire
   body until the magnetic compass needle aligns inside the north

Correcting for Magnetic Declination

First, let me point out you shouldn't need to read this. As long as you adopt one of two sensible approaches to GPS navigation, you should never need to do mental arithmetic to correct for declination. My recommendation is to buy a magnetic compass with adjustable declination, set it to the local declination, and set your GPS receiver to display true bearings. Alternatively, you can buy an inexpensive magnetic compass without adjustable declination and set your GPS receiver to display magnetic bearings. Either way, as long as your compass and your GPS receiver are aligned, you don't have to worry about declination.

If you still want to know how to do the math, read on. The situation we will describe assumes you are using an inexpensive compass without a declination adjustment, and you have set your GPS receiver to read true bearings. (If you're using an adjustable compass that is set to local declination, don't argue, just set your GPS receiver to read true bearings.)

The rules are simple, if you can remember them. To convert the true bearing reported by your GPS receiver into a magnetic bearing, do the following:

If your magnetic declination is East, *subtract* declination
If your magnetic declination is West, *add* declination

This is the origin of the mnemonic "East is least, west is best." East being "least" means you subtract declination; and with a little stretch of your imagination, you can say that west being "best" means you add declination.

Let's take an example. Suppose you are in southern Utah, where the magnetic declination is 13° East. Your GPS receiver tells you your destination waypoint lies at a true bearing of 155°. To convert this to a magnetic bearing, subtract 13°. This gives you a magnetic bearing of 142°.

Now suppose you are in Vermont, where the magnetic declination is 15° West. In this case, you have to add 15°. If your GPS receiver reports a true bearing of 155°, then the magnetic bearing is 170°.

If this isn't complicated enough, it gets worse. Let's suppose you're out in the wilderness and see an interesting mountain peak in the distance. You want to identify it on the map, so you take a compass reading to measure its bearing. Thanks to your GPS receiver you know exactly where you are on the map, so you can just draw a line on the map at the correct bearing angle from your current location to see which peak it intersects. Seems simple enough!

Well, if you don't have a compass with adjustable declination, you'll be reading a magnetic bearing. Unfortunately, the map is aligned with true north, so you have to correct the bearing before you plot the line on the map. In this case, though, the situation is reversed. If your declination is East, you have to add declination to the compass reading to get a true bearing. If it's West, you have to subtract. It's enough to make seasoned hikers want to do all their hiking in the Midwest, where declination is close enough to zero that you don't have to worry about it!

reference indicator. The direction-of-travel indicator is now pointing toward your destination.

3. When returning to your destination, follow the guidelines for Common-Sense Navigation on Page 52.

For some people, this may be all you need to know about GPS navigation. If you only want to find your way back to your starting point or store the locations of places you've already been to, you don't need to worry about things like latitude and longitude or how to enter coordinates from a map. Knowing how to mark and go to waypoints may be all you need. But if not, the next chapters will show you how to use a GPS receiver in more ambitious journeys.

PART 2:
Intermediate Navigation

Key Concepts in Part 2

· Basics of latitude and longitude
· Position formats and datums
· How to enter waypoint coordinates into a GPS receiver
· Basics of geocaching

4
Knowing your Position: Latitude and Longitude

I F YOU WANT TO USE GPS to do more than just return to places you've already been, you'll need to know how to enter waypoints into your receiver without actually going to them. To do this, you first need to understand latitude and longitude. That's what we will cover in this chapter. In Chapter 5 we'll see how to enter waypoint coordinates into your receiver.

Latitude and longitude defined

You might already be somewhat familiar with the concept of latitude and longitude. It's a way to describe your position anywhere on earth. Originally developed by sailors to guide them across oceans, it divides the earth into lines of *latitude*, which indicate how far north or

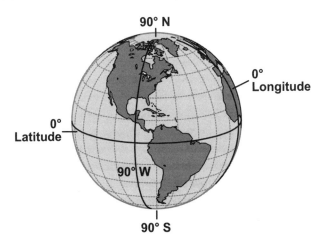

Latitude and longitude are used to define your position anywhere on earth.

south of the equator you are, and lines of *longitude*, which indicate how far east or west of the prime meridian you are.

The equator is defined as 0 degrees latitude, the north pole as 90 degrees *north latitude*, and the south pole as 90 degrees *south latitude*. A complete description of latitude must always include the hemisphere–either north or south. If you just report a latitude as 34 degrees without indicating the hemisphere, you could equally be describing the latitude of Los Angeles, California or Santiago, Chile! All locations in the United States are north latitude.

Latitude lines are always parallel to the equator, so they are called *parallels*. They become smaller in diameter as you move north or south from the equator, but the distance between them remains the same regardless of where you are on the globe.

Longitude lines are called *meridians*. They are circles perpendicular to latitude that run from pole to pole. Unlike latitude, all lines of longitude are the same diameter. They are called *great circles* because they are the largest diameter circles you can draw on a sphere. Longitude lines all come together at the poles, so the distance between them gets smaller as you move away from the equator.

Longitude doesn't have a convenient natural reference point equivalent to the equator for latitude. So the location of 0 degrees of longitude, called the *prime meridian*, is entirely arbitrary. Since the English were the dominant navigators of the 18th century, they chose to define it as the line that runs through the Royal Observatory at Greenwich, England. With only minor changes and the objections of the French notwithstanding, this definition was officially adopted at the 1884 International Meridian Conference in Washington, DC. The recalcitrant French, though, pouted for another 27 years before they grudgingly abandoned their beloved Paris as the site of their prime meridian.

Longitude is a number from 0 to 180 degrees east or west of the prime meridian. Any individual longitude line is only half a circle that runs down one hemisphere from the north pole to the south pole. The other half of the same circle, running up from the south pole to the north pole, is different in number and opposite in hemisphere. As with latitude, don't forget to specify the hemisphere, either east or west. In the United States, all lines of longitude are west longitude.

Position formats

Let's look at how you could describe a position in latitude and longitude. For our example, we'll use the location of the famous Delicate Arch at Arches National Park, Utah. Delicate Arch is north of the equator at latitude 38 degrees, 44 minutes, 37 seconds. It's west of the prime meridian, at longitude 109 degrees, 29 minutes, 58 seconds. When describing a position, latitude comes first. You can write the hemisphere either before or after the number. Most people put it in front. Here's how it would look:

N38° 44′ 37″

W109° 29′ 58″

This is the commonly-used position format known as hemisphere-degrees-minutes-seconds. It's similar to how we describe time. Each degree is divided into 60 minutes and each minute is further subdi-

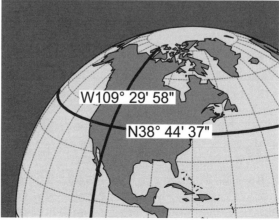

Latitude and longitude of Delicate Arch, Arches National Park, Utah.

vided into 60 seconds. A degree of latitude represents a distance of about 69 miles anywhere on earth, so 1 second of latitude represents a distance of 101 feet. For longitude it's not quite as simple. The distance between lines of longitude decreases as you move north or south of the equator. In the United States, for example, 1 second of longitude ranges from about 87 feet in Jacksonville, Florida, to about 64 feet in Seattle, Washington. Many GPS receivers can display latitude and longitude to a tenth of a second resolution. That's a resolution of about 10 feet in latitude and, for US locations, between 6 and 9 feet in longitude.

Although the degree-minute-second format is commonly used, there are other formats, and you need to know how to tell the difference. If your friend gives you the location of a geocache in one format, for example, and you think it's in another, you'll never find it. One of the most common errors made by experts and novices alike is to incorrectly identify the latitude-longitude format of a position they have been given.

A second position format, known as hemisphere-degrees-decimal minutes, is becoming increasingly popular. It is the preferred format for reporting geocaches. In this format, the number of seconds are converted to fractional numbers of minutes. (You do this by dividing the number of seconds by 60 and adding the result to the number of minutes.) The position of Delicate Arch in the hemisphere-degrees-decimal minutes format looks like this:

N38° 44.611′

W109° 29.971′

A third, less common position format is known as hemisphere-decimal degrees. It goes one step further and converts the number of minutes into fractions of a degree. Again, divide decimal minutes by 60 and add the result to the number of degrees. This is what the position of Delicate Arch looks like in the hemisphere-decimal degrees format:

N38.74351°

W109.49951°

If you've been given GPS coordinates from someone else or have gotten them from a book or the Internet, make sure you understand their position format. It's easy to get confused because many times the symbols for degrees, minutes, and seconds aren't written down. In that case you have to figure it out by looking. If it is a set of three numbers separated by spaces you know it is degrees-minutes-seconds. This is true even if the last number has a decimal point with a number after it—this is just fractions of a second. If it's a set of two numbers, the second having a decimal point and subsequent digits, you know it is the degrees-decimal minutes format. And if it's just one number with a decimal point and subsequent digits, you know it's the decimal degrees format. To further confuse things, on some computer printouts you'll see just a single long number of six or seven digits without any spaces or decimal points. This is a short-form method for the degrees-minutes-seconds format. Computers also often represent north and east by "+" signs and south and west by"-" signs.

Your receiver can select between the different latitude-longitude formats, along with a number of other position formats. Here's how the different latitude-longitude choices are displayed:

Format	Garmin	Magellan
Deg-min-sec	hddd°mm's.s"	DEG.MIN.SEC
Deg-decimal min	hddd°mm.mmm'	DEG.MIN.MMM
Decimal degrees	hddd.ddddd°	DEG.DDDDD

Once you select a position format, your receiver automatically converts the coordinates of any existing waypoints to the new format. But if you're entering new waypoints, you need to make sure your receiver is set to the correct position format *before* you begin to en-

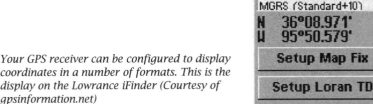

Your GPS receiver can be configured to display coordinates in a number of formats. This is the display on the Lowrance iFinder (Courtesy of gpsinformation.net)

ter numbers. This is another very common mistake that can result in large errors. *Remember: your receiver always assumes that any new waypoint is being entered in the currently-defined position format.* Once the data is entered, your receiver always maintains a waypoint at the same physical location on earth regardless of how you later change formats. The only way to correct a mistake is to first set your receiver to the correct position format and then re-enter the data.

To drive the point home, let's go back to the example of Delicate Arch. Recall that in the degrees-minutes-second format, the latitude of Delicate Arch is:

N38° 44' 37"

Now suppose you didn't realize your receiver was set to degrees-decimal minutes format and you used the above data to incorrectly enter its latitude as:

N38° 44.370'

(the same digits but the wrong format) instead of the correct value, N38° 44.611'. You've just introduced an error of about 1500 feet! You can't fix the problem by switching your receiver to the degrees-minutes-seconds format after you have entered the data. You have to first set the correct position format, then go back and edit the coordinates to the correct numbers.

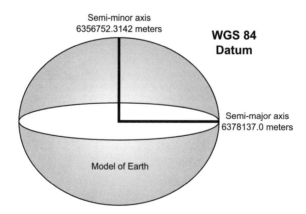

The WGS 84 datum uses an ellipsoidal model of the earth referenced to its center. The older NAD 27 datum uses a different reference, so the same latitude and longitude coordinates represent a different physical location.

Know how to change your receiver's active datum. On this eTrex Vista, you make the selection from the UNITS page.

Map datum

So far, we've been talking about latitude and longitude coordinates as if position format is your only worry. But there's another factor as well: the *datum* used as the horizontal reference. What's a datum? Well, think back to when you learned geography in school. You might vaguely remember your teacher saying the world is not exactly round, it's really an oval with a bulge in the middle caused by the earth's rotation. The distance from the north pole to the south pole is about 13 miles less than it would be if the earth were a perfect sphere. This might not seem like much, but it presents a bit of a problem for latitude and longitude because they are designed for use on a true sphere. Without correcting for this difference you'd get noticeable errors when calculating bearings and distances.

So a datum is a model of the earth. Many different datums[1] have been used over the years by different countries. The two most important for the United States are the North American Datum of 1927, known as NAD 27, and the World Geodetic Survey of 1984, known as WGS 84. These datums represent the earth as an ellipsoid, which is just a fancy name for an oval. The global positioning system was designed around the WGS 84 datum, but many older topographic maps use NAD 27. Always check your map to see which one it uses. The two datums use slightly different models of the earth, so a latitude and longitude expressed with reference to the WGS 84 datum can be as much as 600 feet away from the same coordinates referenced to NAD 27.

---

[1] *Yes, the correct plural for the geographic sense of the word is* datums, *not* data.

You should always verify the datum setting in your receiver. You'll usually find it in one of the menus under the Setup page. There will be only one choice for WGS 84 (it may also list NAD 83, which is a virtually identical datum), but there may be many choices under NAD 27. If so, you will want the one labeled NAD 27 CONUS for "continental United States." The other NAD 27 choices are regional variations. There will also be many other choices, with strange names like "Viti Levu 1916" and "Timbalai 1948." Unless you are an archaeologist using antiquated maps or you travel extensively outside the United States, you'll probably never use most of them.

5
Entering and Navigating to Stored Waypoints

ONCE YOU UNDERSTAND latitude and longitude, you're ready to step up to the next level of navigation skills: programming the coordinates of a waypoint into your GPS receiver without first going to that location. In this chapter we'll assume you have obtained the coordinates from a friend, the Internet or another published source. If so, all you need to know is how to enter them into your receiver. Later, in Chapter 8, you will learn the more advanced technique of plotting your own course by reading coordinates from a map.

Geocaching is a typical example of the kind of navigation we will cover here. Geocaching web sites provide the locations of thousands of caches hidden throughout the world by people like you and me. Fans of the sport log on to one of these sites and use its search tool to get a list of all the caches in their immediate area. They then record the waypoint coordinates for any sites of interest and enter them into their receiver. Much of the fun comes in using the receiver to guide them to the cache. The rest comes from discovering the prizes contained within. We'll cover geocaching in more detail in the next chapter. Here, we'll see how to enter coordinates into your receiver and how to navigate more complex routes.

Obtaining waypoint coordinates

The first step is to obtain the coordinates of the places you want to go. For geocachers, this is easy. There are numerous web sites listing the exact WGS 84 latitudes and longitudes of thousands of hidden caches. You just need to copy down the coordinates of a likely cache and enter them into your receiver.

If you're not a geocacher, you'll have to look elsewhere. Books are one possible source. Hiking guides often publish coordinates for trailside campsites or other points of interest. The Internet can also be useful well beyond geocaching. Numerous sites give you co-ordinates of just about any place you can think of throughout the world. Internet sites come and go with great regularity, so rather than publishing a list here, I'll recommend two sites that will probably be around awhile. The first is a page that provides links to many way-point lists, part of the outstanding *gpsinformation.net* website main-tained by Joe Mehaffey, Jack Yeatzel, and Dale DePriest. You'll find the list of links at: http://gpsinformation.net/main/waypts-2.htm.

The other is the Geographic Names Information System, or GNIS, operated by the US Geological Survey. It can give you the latitudes and longitudes for over 2 million place names in the United States and territories. The GNIS home page is http://geonames.usgs.gov/in-dex.html. From there, go to the Query page.

Strangely, the USGS site does not indicate the map datum for the reported latitude-longitude coordinates. Be aware it is NAD 27. At some point in the future they intend to change over to NAD 83, a da-tum virtually identical to WGS 84, but this is not high on their current

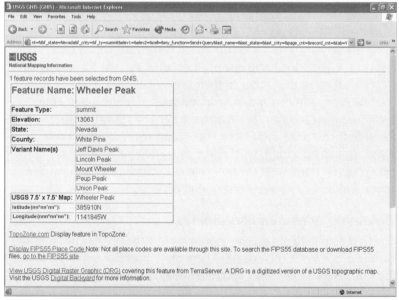

The US Geological Survey web site provides the ability to find latitude and lon-gitude coordinates of 2 million physical and cultural geographic features within the United States and its territories.

priority list. Also be aware the coordinates are read from USGS 7.5-minute topo maps, so they may only be accurate to 5 seconds—about 500 feet in latitude, a bit less in longitude.

Virtually all waypoint coordinates you are likely to come across are reported as latitudes and longitudes. Very rarely you may come across waypoints described in an arcane format known as Universal Transverse Mercator, or UTM. We will briefly describe UTM in Chapter 7. Long-time backcountry hikers sometimes prefer UTM, but it's rare to come across a UTM waypoint that doesn't also indicate its equivalent latitude and longitude. Your GPS receiver knows how to convert from UTM to latitude-longitude and back, so even if you don't understand the UTM system, you can still use it. Just set your receiver's position format to UTM and enter the number/letter combinations exactly as given. Once you've done that, you can switch your receiver back to latitude-longitude if you like.

Organizing waypoint coordinates

Once you have the coordinates for all the waypoints you want to program into your receiver, you need to do some basic housekeeping chores:

1. Determine the map datum for the coordinates. This will usually be either WGS 84 or NAD 27. If you have multiple waypoints with a mix of datums, group all the WGS 84 waypoints together in one set and all the NAD 27 waypoints together in a second set.
2. Verify the position format for the coordinates. It will usually be either hemisphere-degrees-decimal minutes or hemisphere-degrees-minutes-seconds. Again, if you have a mix of formats, group all of one format together in one set, all the others into another set. In the worst case, if you have a mix of both datums and both position formats, you could have four separate sets of waypoints.
3. Decide on the name you want to assign to each waypoint, and write it next to its waypoint coordinates. Check to see if a waypoint of the same name already exists in the receiver's database. If so, just edit the coordinates of that waypoint rather than creating a new waypoint from scratch.

Programming waypoint coordinates

Now you're ready to enter the data into your GPS receiver. If you have multiple waypoints the process can take awhile, so make sure

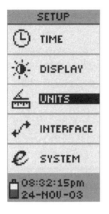

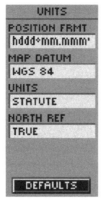

The map datum and position format are usually accessed from the Setup page. This receiver's position format is set to DEGREES-DECIMAL MINUTES and its map datum to WGS 84.

the batteries in your receiver are fresh. It's not necessary to be locked onto satellites when entering waypoints, so you can do this job indoors. In fact, even if you are outside, you will save considerable battery power by setting your receiver to the "GPS Off" mode (Sometimes called "Demo"), a choice usually found on the Setup page. That way you aren't draining your batteries by powering up the actual receiver electronics when they're not being used.

Before entering the data, go to your receiver's setup page and check the setting for both the map datum and the position format. If either of them isn't the same format as your data, make the change now. Remember you have to correctly set your receiver before you begin entering data, otherwise you'll have to go back and do it again.

You'd think that manufacturers would make it easy to enter waypoints by providing a choice labeled something like "CREATE WAYPOINT." But few receivers provide such a key. Instead, you have to use the same MARK key you use to store your current position, then remember to edit the location before you save it. The actual process varies by receiver, so study your instruction manual for specific details. The general sequence looks like this:

1. Call up the MARK page.
2. Highlight the waypoint's number and change it to the chosen name.
3. Highlight the latitude-longitude coordinates and edit them to the correct position.
4. If your receiver allows you to select from a set of symbols, you may want to change the symbol to another choice—a tent symbol

On many receivers, when you want to manually enter the position coordinates of a new waypoint you must first call up the MARK WAYPOINT screen as if you were going to store your present position. Then before storing it, you must change the position coordinates to the desired location.

for a campsite or a car symbol for the location of your parked car, for example. The advantage of doing this is that you can later go back and delete all the waypoints having a common symbol without affecting other types of waypoints.

5. Some receivers allow you to enter an elevation for the waypoint. This is not a necessary input, so unless you are sure you know it, leave it blank.

6. Store the waypoint by selecting SAVE (Magellan and Cobra receivers) or OK (Garmin receivers).

7. Repeat the process for each additional waypoint.

If all your waypoints use the same datum and position formats, you can just enter them one after another. If not, you first need to enter those that match the receiver's current formats, then go back to

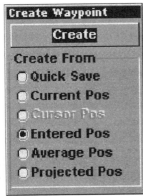

The Lowrance iFinder is one of the few receivers that provides the explicit option of creating a waypoint by entering a position. (Courtesy of gpsinformation.net)

the setup page and change the datum or position format as necessary to enter the remaining waypoints.

No matter what GPS receiver you own, entering waypoints directly from the front panel is so cumbersome you'll soon want to find an easier way. If you own a computer with a serial port, you can make the job much easier. All you need is the right software package. In addition to the mapping software programs we will discuss in Chapter 7, you can use *EasyGPS*, a free program you can download from the TopoGrafix web site at http://www.easygps.com. The free version gives rather limited capability: your waypoints must be referenced to WGS 84 and you can't download tracks. Purchasing the expert upgrade gives you many additional features including NAD 27 and tracklog capability.

Navigating to stored waypoints

You navigate to a manually-programmed waypoint using the same approach as described in Chapter 3. First select the GOTO function to find the bearing and distance to the waypoint. Then use your compass to determine where that direction actually is. Head in the indicated direction, subject to the limitations of the terrain. The same cautions also apply: don't blindly head straight across uncertain terrain. Instead, pick a route that gets you in the general direction without undue risk or damage to the environment. Go around obstacles, not over them. Check your receiver occasionally to get an updated bearing and adjust your course accordingly. And keep your eyes focused on your surroundings, not your receiver. Pick a target object like a tree or boulder in the distance and use it as an intermediate

If you have a mapping receiver you can use its internal map to get an idea of a destination's location. The built-in base map probably won't be sufficient, you'll need to download a more detailed map from your receiver manufacturer's map software program. This Garmin Rino has been loaded with data from the MapSource Topo software. No software map is without error. The correct name of the lake shown on this map is Ilsanjo.

goal. When you get to it, use your receiver to update the bearing to your destination and continue the process until you arrive. If you're not sure how to follow a bearing, go back and read Chapter 3 in detail.

One added complication is that you often won't have a good idea of where your target waypoint is actually located. If it's a hidden geo-cache, for instance, you might not even know exactly where to park to begin your search. More than once I've parked at what I thought was a good starting point only to find my way blocked by fence lines, cliffs, or rows of houses. So it's a good idea to at least get a general idea of the waypoint's location before you start out.

There are several ways to do this. If you own a highway or topo-graphic mapping software program that runs on a personal com-puter, you can enter the waypoint coordinates from the keyboard and view its location on the map display. Zoom in to get a reasonable idea of how to get to the waypoint. We'll cover the subject of software maps in detail in Chapter 8.

Another option is to use an online mapping service. Two good free sources are TopoZone at http://www.topozone.com and Maptech at http://mapserver.maptech.com/homepage/index.cfm. You'll learn more about TopoZone in Chapter 6. With Maptech, select the "Advanced Search" option and enter the waypoint coordinates in either degrees-minutes-seconds or decimal degrees. If using decimal degrees make sure to enter a "-" sign in front of longitude to repre-sent the western hemisphere.

The result will be a digital USGS 7.5-minute map of the general area, but the desired spot won't necessarily be at the center of the page. Move the cursor while watching the latitude-longitude displays until it is over the desired position.

The Maptech server uses the NAD 27 format, so if your waypoints are referenced to WGS 84 you need to convert them. This is easy enough to do. Just enter them into your receiver in WGS 84 format, then change the receiver's map datum to NAD 27. The coordinates of your waypoints will now be displayed in NAD 27 format. Be sure to set the datum back to WGS 84 when finished.

The free EasyGPS program described above also has the ability to link directly to the Maptech server. It places a crosshair at the way-point's location on the online map.

Finally, you have the tried and true option of using paper maps. You'll need one with a latitude and longitude scale such as a USGS topo map. It's a little more difficult to get an accurate reading from a paper map, but you can easily get a general idea just by looking. Often that's enough to get you to a good starting point. If you need more precise information, we'll cover the subject of reading latitudes and longitudes from topo maps in Chapter 8.

6
Geocaching

GEOCACHING IS A FAST-GROWING new sport that's a great way to practice GPS navigation skills. The concept is simple. One person hides a container that typically includes a log book, instruction sheet, and a few trading items—the *cache*—and posts its latitude and longitude coordinates on an Internet web site. Other people look up the coordinates of the cache on the web, then use their GPS receivers to try to find it. When they do, they sign the log book and if they want, take an item. According to geocaching etiquette, if you take an item you must leave another item to replace it. When finished, the cache (pronounced *cash)* is returned to its hiding place for others to find.

It sounds easier than it is. Remember your receiver is typically only accurate to about 20 or 30 feet, and the cache is often camouflaged and small. Your receiver will only get you into the general area. It's up to you to search around until you find it.

Geocaching was unheard of before the government turned off Selective Availability in the year 2000. But within days the first cache

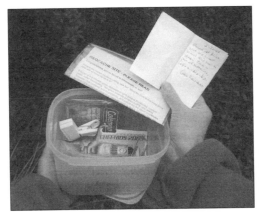

A typical geocache consists of a waterproof container holding a log book, instruction sheet, and inexpensive trading items.

was planted in Oregon and the sport was off and running. Now it is a worldwide phenomenon with caches in nearly 200 countries. Hiding spots range from locations far in the wilderness to downtown urban areas. Geocachers run the gamut from dedicated enthusiasts who hike miles in the backcountry to parents and children who go no farther than the local park.

The first caches were fairly large army surplus ammo boxes, but these days almost any container is used. I've seen fake hollow rocks, magnetic keyholders, and just about every kind of plastic or rubber container you can imagine. Hollow logs and rock piles seem to be favorite hiding places. A cache placed in the wilderness need not be well camouflaged, but in an urban area the biggest challenge is hiding it in a way it won't be found by non-geocachers (called *geomuggles* in geocaching lingo, after the non-magical "muggles" from the *Harry Potter* stories).

Most caches are placed on public lands, although with the owner's permission they can be placed on private property. Some government agencies—viewing geocaches as little more than trash, or fearful of potential environmental damage from legions of geocachers tramping willy-nilly over the hillsides—have banned geocaching within

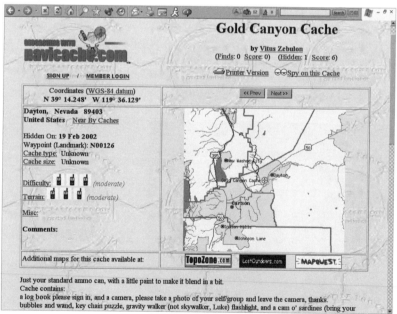

Typical cache page on Navicache.com. (Courtesy of Navicache.com)

their jurisdiction. The National Park Service falls into this category. Other agencies recognize the sport as a way to get more people out to enjoy nature and appreciate their parks. Before you hide a cache on public land make sure you are not in violation of any government regulation.

Geocaching web sites

Before you can find a cache, you need to know where to look. The two most important geocaching Internet sites are Geocaching.com at http://www.geocaching.com and Navicache.com at http://www. navicache.com. These sites provide the coordinates for thousands of hidden caches. Both provide free access, although Geocaching.com also offers what they call a "Premium Membership" that gives you, for a fee, early notification of new caches and access to otherwise unpublished caches. Navicache takes a different approach based on the premise of complete free access to the site. Both provide many opportunities for a good hunt.

If you prefer to find cache coordinates by way of a map rather than entering Zip codes or latitudes and longitudes, check out Buxley's Geocaching Waypoint at http://www.brillig.com/geocaching. This

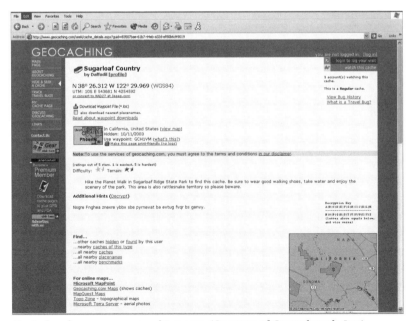

Typical cache page on geocaching.com. (Courtesy of Groundspeak, Inc.)

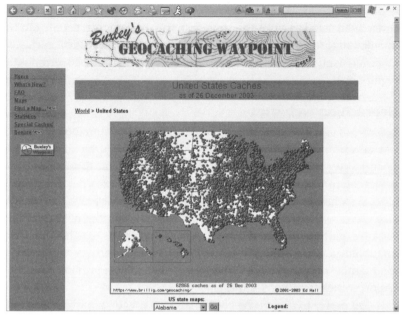

Buxley's Geocaching Waypoint allows you to search for caches using a map.
(Courtesy of Ed Hall)

"search-engine" page provides map-based links to the caches on the Navicache.com and Geocaching.com web pages.

An Internet search on the words "geocaching" or "geocache" will turn up hundreds of other web sites, including regional and international geocaching organizations, upcoming events, and various words of advice. If you're new to the sport, it might be worthwhile to spend a little time browsing a few such sites to learn more about it.

Cache types

Geocaching is so new the rules of the game are still evolving. There are several generally-accepted types of caches:

Regular cache. The original type of cache, also called a *normal* cache. It includes a log book and prizes in a container roughly the size of a breadbox. Army-surplus ammo boxes were the original favorite containers, but too many people considered the boxes themselves to be neat prizes and carted them away. So now you are more likely to see things like Rubbermaid containers, old peanut-butter jars, or empty paint buckets. Caches placed in containers about the size of a

5-gallon paint can are known as *large* caches.

Micro cache. Similar to a regular cache but much smaller. Film canisters, magnetic keyholders, and empty breath-mint tins are examples. Often there is little room for anything other than the logbook.

Offset cache. This is a little more complicated than the standard cache. The published coordinates direct you to some sort of point of interest. You must then continue to a nearby location based on information you learn at the site or given on the cache's web page.

Multi-part caches. This type requires that you find multiple caches to complete your quest. In one version, several caches are posted on the Internet. Each cache you visit gives you a piece of information necessary to find a final, unpublished cache. In another version each successive cache gives you coordinates to the next cache in a sequence.

Virtual cache. In urban or heavily-traveled rural areas it isn't always possible to place a physical cache. The base of Yosemite Falls, for example, sees so many visitors it would be impossible to keep a cache hidden for long even if it weren't against park regulations. A virtual cache gives you the coordinates of a particular point of interest and asks you to answer a question about the location. You e-mail the answer to the "owner" of the cache to prove you were there. This is the only type of cache currently permitted in national parks.

Geocaching rules

Here are the most important rules of the sport:

1. If you take an item from the cache, leave an item. Check Rule 6 below for information on what *not* to put in a cache.
2. Record your visit in the log book.
3. Put the cache back in the same place you found it, unless its instructions say otherwise.
4. Report your visit on the web site where you found the coordinates.

If you plan to hide a cache, there are some additional considerations:

5. Be sure to include a log book so visitors can record their experiences. If there's room, include a pencil. If not, be sure your on-line description of the cache tells people to bring their own.
6. Use common sense when stocking your cache. Never put anything

dangerous like fireworks, explosives, ammunition, weapons such
as knives, alcohol, illegal substances, or pornography. Remember
that geocaching is a family sport and children are often the first
to find a cache, so plan accordingly. Food items are also strongly
discouraged. Animals are more likely than humans to benefit from
such treasures. Besides, would you really want to sample a choco-
late bar that may have sat out in the elements for who knows how
many months? If you want to provide food, do so with gift certificates for free hamburgers or ice cream cones at a local restaurant.

7. Never bury a cache. The sport is based on a premise of minimiz-
   ing environmental impact, so it needs to be placed where it can be
   found with minimal damage to the environment.

8. When you place a cache, you become its "owner." You are responsible for visiting it on occasion to make sure it is in good repair
   and that the area around it doesn't show signs of overuse. Remove
   a cache if the environmental impact becomes more than minimal.
   For this reason, you shouldn't place a cache while on vacation or in
   a remote area you can't regularly return to.

9. Make sure to record the correct GPS coordinates. Use the WGS 84
   datum, and in general, use the degrees-decimal minutes format.
   Turn on averaging, if available in your receiver, to improve the
   waypoint's accuracy. Check the rules of the specific web site for
   additional information.

Finding a cache

If you're new to geocaching, the first thing you should do is practice
finding caches. This allows you to learn the general principles of the
sport before you start hiding caches of your own. From the home
pages at either Navicache.com or Geocaching.com you can enter a Zip
code to get a listing of all caches in the immediate area. The sites also
have advanced capabilities that allow you to search on latitude-longitude coordinates, cache names, and several other criteria.

The result of your search will be a list of nearby caches, including hyperlinks to the individual cache pages. Click on a link to learn
about a specific cache. Here you will see its latitude-longitude coordinates (geocaching.com also provides UTM coordinates), learn more
about the cache, and read the log notes recorded by previous visitors.
Pick a cache that sounds appealing and enter its coordinates into
your receiver. Now you're ready to go find it.

Preparation. The web page for a cache defaults to a high-level map of the surrounding area. It might not be detailed enough to show where to start your hunt. You want to avoid starting from a spot that appears close only to find the way blocked by a canyon, housing development, oil refinery, etc. So it's a good idea to study a more detailed map before you head out. Geocaching.com and Navicache.com both give you the option to display the cache location on other online maps including TopoZone, MapQuest, and Microsoft Maps. Topo maps are good bet for caches hidden in rural areas. Street maps are best for urban caches. And this is one area where a mapping receiver really shines. With the right detailed map loaded in memory, you can let your receiver guide you directly from your home to the jumping-off point.

If you're going to a cache that's off the beaten path, you will want to prepare the same way you would for any serious hike. Assemble a backpack with a few basic items: GPS receiver, extra batteries (very important!), magnetic compass, water, snacks, first-aid kit, and perhaps a jacket or windbreaker. A cell phone can be handy if you will

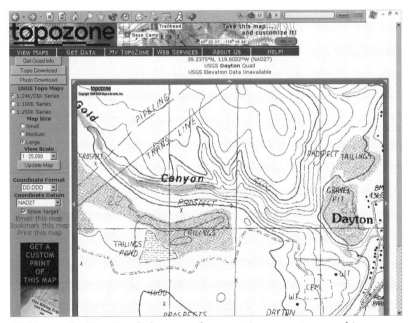

Clicking on the TopoZone link on a cache page gives you a topographic map of the cache location. You can also access TopoZone directly at www.topozone. com. (Copyright 1999-2003 Maps a la carte, Inc.)

be within its coverage area. And don't forget to include items you can use to trade! If you plan to be a geocaching regular, you may want to keep the kit together permanently so you can head out at a moment's notice.

Search. It can be just as hard to find the right parking spot for your car as it is to find the cache. Some cache web pages will give you at least an idea of where to start from, but in many cases you're on your own. If you studied a map before you started, you should be able to get reasonably close. Park your car and turn on your GPS receiver to get a position fix. The first thing to do, if the cache is any significant distance away, is to *mark the location of your car as a waypoint.* You don't want to get yourself into the unenviable position of having found the cache but having no idea how to get back! Remember the Cardinal Rule of GPS Navigation: *it doesn't do you any good to know where you are if you don't know where you want to go.*

We've already covered the topic of navigating with a GPS receiver, so we won't repeat it here. If you have any questions, now would be a good time to go back and review the basics starting on Page 52.

Many geocachers keep their GPS receivers turned on for the duration of the quest. That way they can use the compass page as their primary navigation tool. Ever since the demise of Selective Availability the compass page has become reasonably useful even at walking speeds. It's still a good idea to carry a magnetic compass as a back-up and for use when you are standing still.

Be sure to check the satellite status page occasionally. If you are navigating through forests or canyons, your receiver could lose lock on a satellite or two and drop back into 2D mode. If so, your indicated position could be hundreds of feet away from your actual position. Move around as necessary to keep your receiver operating in 3D mode.

The last 15-20 feet are the most challenging. At this point it's best to put your receiver away—it won't be able to help you now. This is where your search skills become important. Try to imagine where you would have hidden the cache if it was yours. Hollow logs, rock piles, and clumps of brush all make likely hiding spots. The rules of geocaching prohibit buried caches, so don't dig up the ground. But caches are often loosely covered with twigs, small rocks, or dried grass, so check around.

Use common sense when checking concealed spots. It is always possible that snakes, spiders, or scorpions could be lurking within. I've found it useful to carry a hiking staff that I first use to probe such areas. And you should always keep an eye out for poison oak, poison ivy, poison sumac, or whatever other poisonous plants are native to the surrounding area.

At the cache. Once you've spotted the cache and before you retrieve it, look around to see if anyone else is nearby. You don't want a geomuggle to accidentally discover and pillage the cache after you've left. Wait until it's safe, then retrieve it. Record your visit in the log, swap items if you want, then seal the cache and replace it where you found it. Don't forget to log your visit on the web page when you return home.

Hiding a cache

Eventually after you have found a few caches you may want to hide your own. Re-read the above rules for hiding caches, then decide on a plan. At first you will probably want to keep things simple by hiding a regular cache. Do some research before hiding it. Are there already other caches nearby? To minimize environmental impact, cache websites ususally won't accept new caches placed too close to an existing cache. Also make sure your intended site doesn't violate laws or property rights. Don't place a cache on private property without the owner's permission. On public lands, check with the managing agency if you aren't sure of their policy toward geocaching.

You'll also have to decide how difficult you want to make the search. A cache that's easy to reach will receive more visits than one placed far in the wilderness. But the challenge of the find can make the wilderness cache a more rewarding experience for those who attempt it. Also give consideration to how the cache is hidden. Don't make people scramble across a delicate natural environment to get to it. The best caches are ones that give the visitor another reason to be there besides the cache—a great scenic view or historical point of interest, for example. Check the web site where you plan to post the cache for any additional rules they may have.

Remember your cache will lie exposed to the weather year round, so choose a container suitable for the environment. If possible, use a plastic or metal container having an airtight seal. Avoid easily-broken glass jars. Label the container as a geocache according to instructions on the appropriate web page, so that if it's accidentally found by a

Travel bug.

geomuggle they won't think it's trash and dispose of it.

So far we've discussed what not to put in a cache, but equally important is what to put in. You don't need to spend a lot of money. Cheap toys are great, since many geocachers are children. Other common items include cash (coins or paper), CDs, DVDs, gift certificates, sunscreen, books, or just about anything else you can think of. Use your imagination. Some cache owners include single-use disposable cameras. The idea is for visitors to take their pictures at the cache and leave the camera there. When all the shots are exposed, the cache owner develops the film and posts the photos on the web.

Travel bugs

A *travel bug* (also called a *hitchhiker*) is an item intended to travel from one cache to another. The item can be anything—toys and stuffed animals are favorites—but what distinguishes it is a coded metal tag dangling from it. If you take a travel bug from a cache you're not supposed to keep it but rather place it in another cache and keep it moving. You also need to log onto the web site indicated on the tag to record that you have taken it and to learn whatever instructions the owner has posted for it. The goal might be for the bug to travel around the world or hit as many states as possible in a specific period, so don't hold onto a travel bug for any length of time. As soon as practical, go out to another cache and send it on its way. Then make sure you go to its on-line log and record where you placed it, so the owner can track its journey.

Geocaching can be a great sport for the whole family. Follow the simple guidelines in this chapter and you will have a good excuse to get outside with your GPS receiver more often.

PART 3:
Advanced Navigation

Key Concepts in Part 3

- Basics of topographic maps
- Elevation and contour lines
- The UTM coordinate system
- Basics of software maps
- Planning and navigating GPS routes

7
Topographic Maps

BEFORE YOU CAN DO ANY SERIOUS GPS navigation you need to understand maps. With the right map you can:

- See how to drive to the trailhead
- Plot a course across the land, either along trails or by cross-country bushwhacking
- Find the latitude and longitude of places you want to visit
- Learn the steepness and variability of the terrain you'll be crossing
- Identify obstacles such as rivers or cliffs along your path
- Find your position in the field by comparing physical features of the land to their representations on the map

Not every map is equally useful. The highway maps you pick up at the local supermarket or auto club are examples of what are called *planimetric* maps. They show towns and highways, and perhaps an occasional railroad or river. But they don't show terrain in any detail at all. Sometimes they plot forests in green or deserts in brown, and occasionally they will show the location and elevation of a notable mountain peak. But beyond this you can't tell whether a region is dead flat or steep mountainous terrain. Nor can you read the latitude and longitude of a location. Highway maps are great for showing you how to drive to the trailhead, but are nearly useless once you are actually on the trail. What you need in the wilderness is the kind of map called a *topographic* map.

Topo map basics

A topographic, or "topo" map not only shows natural and manmade features in more detail than a planimetric map, it also displays the physical shape of the terrain. It does this by way of *contour lines* rep-

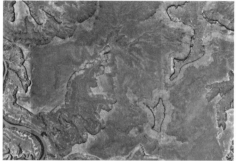

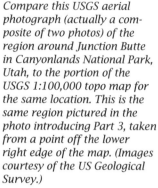

Compare this USGS aerial photograph (actually a composite of two photos) of the region around Junction Butte in Canyonlands National Park, Utah, to the portion of the USGS 1:100,000 topo map for the same location. This is the same region pictured in the photo introducing Part 3, taken from a point off the lower right edge of the map. (Images courtesy of the US Geological Survey.)

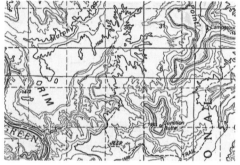

resenting paths of constant elevation of the land. Knowing the contours of the terrain you can determine whether your intended route is relatively flat or will climb 2000 feet. You can also determine how the route changes elevation—a path that repeatedly climbs and then descends 100 feet at a time can be more strenuous than one that slowly but steadily climbs the same amount in a single run.

Contour lines

Most topo maps show contour lines in brown ink. To make them easier to read, every fifth line, called an *index contour*, is printed in bold and its elevation is labeled. Make sure you know whether the numbers are in feet or meters.

You might find it helpful to understand the concept of contour lines by thinking of an egg slicer—that handy kitchen gadget used to cut eggs, grapes, strawberries, and the occasional finger into neat stacks of slices all the same thickness. Imagine a gigantic egg slicer, its cutting wires spaced 40 feet apart, turned sideways so it can slice horizontally through a mountain. If you looked from the top down after it was sliced, the outline of the mountain at each cut would rep-

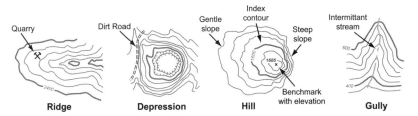

Examples of contour lines and other features found on a topographic map.

resent its contour at that elevation.

Depending on the steepness of the terrain, you might want to change the distance between the cutting wires on your giant egg slicer. In relatively flat areas, 40 feet might not give you enough resolution, so you would want to set the wires only 10 or 20 feet apart. In very steep areas you might want an even greater spacing, perhaps 60 or 80 feet.

In the same way, the contour interval chosen by a map maker will depend on the local topography of the land. Maps covering mountainous areas adopt larger contour intervals than those covering fairly flat regions. You'll always find the contour interval printed somewhere on the map, usually near its scale rule. Pay attention, because it's not always the same even among different maps from the same series. Some US Geological Survey maps, for example, report contour intervals in feet, others in meters.

By studying the shapes of the contour lines you can learn information about the land. Lines that are close together represent steep slopes. Widely spaced lines are gentle slopes. Mountain peaks are represented by concentric rings. V-shaped lines pointing uphill indicate a canyon or gully. V- or U-shaped lines pointing downhill indicate a ridge. To help you interpret the various symbols on a topo map, the United States Geological Survey produces a handy pamphlet entitled *Topographic Map Symbols.* You can get an online copy at: http://erg.usgs.gov/isb/pubs/booklets/symbols/.

Practice reading topo maps by picking up a map of a nearby area. Study the map, then take it along and go out to see how it relates to the physical features of the landscape.

Elevation

Topo maps represent elevation with respect to something called a *vertical datum,* which is the "zero elevation" reference. Usually, this

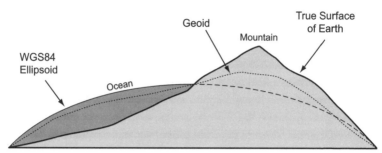

Maps report elevations with reference to mean sea level as defined by the earth's geoid. GPS receivers often measure elevation with respect to the WGS84 ellipsoid, which only approximates mean sea level.

is defined as mean sea level, abbreviated MSL. Seems simple enough, right? Unfortunately, it's not. When you are at the beach, you can easily measure sea level, but if you're at a peak in the Rocky Mountains, you don't have that luxury.

There are two ways to define MSL when you don't have an ocean conveniently located nearby. The first is to define it as the elevation at which the force of gravity is the same as at actual sea level—where sea level would be if the land wasn't in the way. This is the definition used by topo maps. This line of constant gravity, called the *geoid*, is not a flat surface. It varies irregularly depending on the shape of the land and the density of the rocks in the immediate vicinity. The change in local gravity caused by the mass of the mountains actually makes mean sea level higher than it would be if the mountains weren't there.

The other way to define mean sea level is to mathematically model it. Most models represent the earth as an ellipsoid. In this case, MSL is the height of the ellipsoid that best matches the true shape of the earth.

The standard ellipsoid adopted by GPS is the WGS 84 *vertical* datum. (Latitude and longitude reference the WGS 84 *horizontal* datum). Mathematical models are convenient for GPS receivers, but they only approximately represent the true geoid. Depending on your location, there can be a difference of more than 300 feet between the two. Across the continental United States the geoid ranges from about 10 feet above to 100 feet below the WGS 84 ellipsoid.

The scientific community has only recently spent much time trying to understand the earth's geoid. The most current geoid of the continental United States is known as GEOID99. It is based on millions of gravimetric measurements made across the country. Expensive commercial GPS receivers use GEOID99 as their elevation reference, but consumer units often still use the less complicated but also less accurate WGS 84 ellipsoid. This is one reason why GPS elevation accuracy is much worse than horizontal accuracy. You can learn more about GEOID99 by visiting the NOAA web page at: http://www.ngs. noaa.gov/GEOID/GEOID99/.

It's virtually impossible to find out which reference your consumer unit uses. You won't find it in the manufacturers' published literature, and even their online customer support teams don't seem to know.

USGS maps

Topo maps are produced by various government agencies and some private companies. The most comprehensive source is the US Geological Survey. Besides their regional field offices, USGS maps are readily available at many outdoor shops. You can also order them online directly from the USGS website at: http://topomaps.usgs.gov/.

The USGS produces several map series at various scales. The most comprehensive is known as the 7.5-minute series because each map covers 7.5 minutes of latitude by 7.5 minutes of longitude. This is the most useful scale for outdoor recreation. It takes about 57,000 maps to cover the entire United States including Hawaii but excluding Alaska, where 15-minute maps are used. The scale for 7.5-minute maps is 1:24,000, which means that 1 inch on the map represents 24,000 inches, or 2,000 feet, in real life. (A few use a scale of 1:25,000.) These are known as *large scale* maps because they cover a small area (less than 10×10 miles) in great detail. It might sound counterintuitive to call a map "large scale" when it covers a small area, but that's the way it's done. Think of it as large scale because it takes a large sheet of paper to show the same area as a small-scale map shows on a small sheet.

The USGS also produces topo maps at several smaller scales, including 1:100,000, 1:250,000, 1:500,000 and 1:1,000,000. These show larger areas but in less detail than the 7.5-minute series. The USGS used to produce a series of 15-minute maps, but ongoing budget pressures caused these to be discontinued except in Alaska ("abandoned" in USGS parlance, as if they were left off at a homeless shelter somewhere). Fifteen-minute maps of the continental US were drawn at a scale of 1:62,500, where 1 inch represented not quite 1 mile.

Not until Alaska did the USGS settle on the more practical scale of
1:63,360, which looks like a strange number but results in a map
where 1 inch represents *exactly* 1 mile.

Fifteen-minute maps were a convenient scale for hikers, but less
useful for mining and oil exploration, so when cuts had to be made
it was the 15-minute series that was abandoned. Several private companies sell updated versions of the old 15-minute series for national
parks and other popular hiking areas, although they don't always
print them at the standard scale. Remember that USGS maps are often 10 or more years old, so don't depend on them in areas that have
seen recent development. You can learn more about USGS topo maps
online at: http://erg.usgs.gov/mac/isb/pubs/booklets/usgsmaps/
usgsmaps.html.

Understanding topo maps

While the *Topographic Map Symbols* pamphlet will help you understand much about the map, it won't tell you everything. Map borders
are full of information of varying usefulness. Let's look a the most
important information on a USGS 7.5 minute paper map.

Lower Right Margin. This is where you find the name of the map and
its date of publication. There's also a simple legend limited to road
symbols. Newer printings include an ISBN bar code.

Lower Center Margin. Here is the map scale, contour interval, and
the vertical datum reference. Don't confuse the vertical datum, used
only as an elevation reference, with the much more important horizontal datum used as the position reference. Coastal maps also include depth and shoreline information.

Lower Left Margin. Buried among such things as hydrographic data
and grid tick information is the all-important horizontal datum. On
most USGS maps this is the 1927 North American Datum, or NAD
27. Although it doesn't say so, maps of the continental US use what
GPS receivers often call NAD 27 CONUS, whose reference point is a
physical location on the Meades Ranch in Kansas. Some newer maps
also give instructions on how to translate coordinates to the NAD 83
datum, which is virtually identical to WGS 84.

Neatlines. The borders of the map, called *neatlines*, always align with

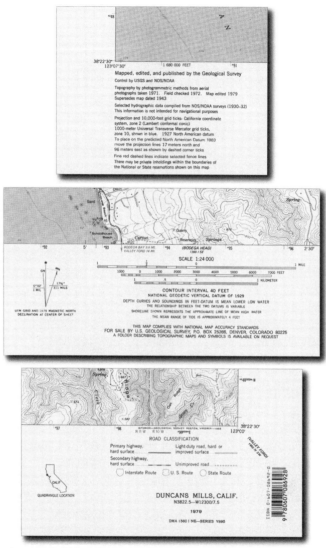

Information on a USGS 7.5' topographic map: lower left margin (top), lower center margin (middle), lower right margin (lbottom).

either an even minute or a 30-second line of latitude or longitude. Along the neatlines are numbers relating to various coordinate systems. Latitude and longitude are shown in degrees-minutes-seconds format. The full numbers are printed at the map corners, but only the minutes and seconds in between. Numbers for other coordinate sys-

tems are interspersed along the neatlines, making it a little difficult
to identify the intermediate latitude and longitude markings. Look
for the numbers with the minutes (') or seconds (") marks after
them.

You can read the latitude and longitude of any point using the
technique described in the next chapter, then enter the coordinates
into your receiver as a GPS waypoint. If you do this very often,
though, you'll probably want to learn the UTM system described below, because UTM coordinates are much easier to read from a paper
map. USGS maps all include blue UTM tic marks along the neatlines,
and some maps have full UTM grids printed in blue. You can recognize UTM labels because the leading one or two digits are printed in
smaller font than the next two digits.

The remaining black tic marks represent the State Plane
Coordinate System. Only the marks nearest the lower left and upper
right corners are labeled, with a number in feet. Don't worry about
these markings. Unless you are a surveyor you will have little need
for them.

Finally, the names of the eight adjacent maps are centered along
the vertical and horizontal neatlines and diagonally in each of the
four corners of the map.

The UTM grid

All maps suffer from a common problem: they must represent the
3-dimensional surface of the earth on a 2-dimensional sheet of paper
or computer screen. No matter how you do it, this introduces some
distortion. We've all seen maps that try to portray the entire world as
a single rectangular sheet, others that cut it into oddly-shaped pieces
like the peels of an orange. Distortions are usually most noticeable
on lines of longitude. While on a 3-dimensional globe all longitude
lines are straight, when they are projected onto on the flat surface of
a map some will be straight, others bent.

As we have also seen, the distance between lines of longitude decreases as you move away from the equator. At the equator, a degree
of longitude spans about 69 miles, while at the arctic circle it is only
about 26 miles. Latitude doesn't suffer this problem. A degree of latitude spans 69 miles everywhere on the globe.

This variation makes it difficult to measure latitude and longitude
coordinates on a map. Special latitude-longitude rulers have been developed, but as you will see in the next chapter they are cumbersome

to use, especially in the field. The Universal Transverse Mercator, or *UTM*, grid was developed as a way to make it easier to determine the coordinates of a location on a paper map. As you might imagine, it has its roots in the military, where a similar grid is known as the *Military Grid Reference System,* or *MGRS.* It is designed for use with large scale maps such as the USGS 7.5 minute series.

The UTM grid divides the entire world from 80 degrees south latitude to 84 degrees north latitude into 60 zones, each covering 6 degrees of longitude. The zones are numbered consecutively, with zone 1 covering the range from 180 degrees to 174 degrees west longitude. Subsequent zones increase in number every six degrees as you move eastward. The continental US is covered by zones 10 through 19. A rectangular metric grid overlays each zone. The grid in each zone is completely independent of those in other zones, making UTM somewhat complicated to use for travels that stretch across multiple zones.

The system is designed so that you read horizontal distances eastward and vertical distances northward from reference lines. Not

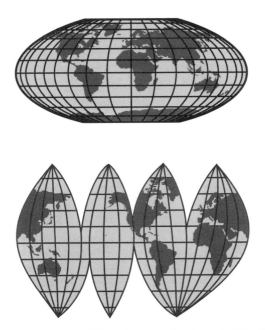

Map makers have used many different approaches to project the 3-dimensional surface of the earth onto a 2-dimensional map. All introduce some level of distortion.

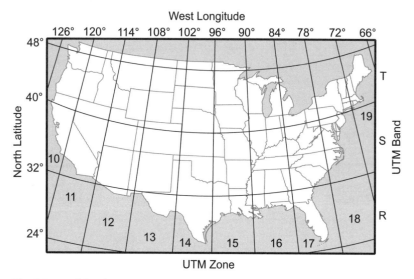

The UTM grid for the continental United States spans Zones 10 through 19 and Bands R through U. Each zone spans 6 degrees of longitude and each band spans 8 degrees of latitude.

surprisingly, these are called *eastings* and *northings*. To measure the coordinates of a location you first read its distance in meters east of a vertical reference line, then north of a horizontal reference line—a process often expressed as "read right, then up."

The center grid line of each zone runs straight along the longitude of its central meridian, 3° away from either border. This line is arbitrarily assigned a value of 500,000 meters so that no matter where in the zone you are, you will always read a positive easting number. For coordinates in the northern hemisphere, the northing origin is defined as the equator. But if you used this approach in the southern hemisphere, all northing measurements would be negative numbers, so for the southern hemisphere, the equator is assigned the value of 10,000,000 meters. To keep you from getting confused as to whether a particular set of coordinates refers to the northern hemisphere or southern hemisphere, each zone is divided horizontally into 20 bands of latitude, each 8 degrees high. The bands are assigned letters from "C" at the extreme south to "X" at the extreme north (this last band is actually 12 degrees high). The full UTM coordinates for a point therefore must include the UTM zone number, the vertical band letter within the zone, and a single long number that is the combination of the easting and northing numbers, like this example:

> 11 S 6456673862920

The "11" means Zone 11, and the "S" means Band S within the zone. The single long number is the combination of the easting and northing. To help decipher it, just remember that the easting number always has one less digit than the northing. So in this example, the easting is 645667 meters and the northing is 3862920 meters. Sometimes you'll see UTM coordinates with fewer digits. This just means there is less resolution to the number. With 13 digits as in the above example, the resolution is 1 meter. With seven digits, the resolution is only 1 kilometer, as in this example:

> 11 S 6463863

Here, the easting is 646 kilometers and the northing is 3863 kilometers.

In an attempt to make it easier to read, the easting and northing numbers are often written on separate lines, like this:

> 11 S 0645667
> 3862920

That's how your GPS receiver shows the numbers. Notice the leading zero on the easting number so both easting and northing have the same number of digits.

Sometimes you'll see UTM coordinates written on a single line with easting and northing spelled out:

> 11 S E645667 N3862920

This is how UTM coordinates are shown on the geocaching.com web page, for example. Just remember the "E" or "N" are only for clarification. You don't actually enter them into your GPS receiver. And you'll probably have to enter a leading zero on the easting number.

Topo maps usually abbreviate the UTM number. Since the tic marks occur on 1000 meter increments, there's no need to show the last 3 zeroes except in the lower left and upper right corners. The digits representing the thousand and ten-thousand meter values are also printed in a larger font. The values in the lower left and upper right corners of the map look like this: $^647000m$ E and $^3862000m$ N. Across the rest of the map, values are abbreviated to look like this: ^{646} and ^{3863}.

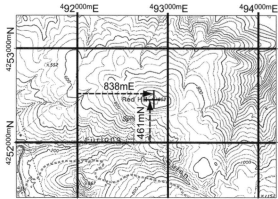

UTM coordinates are designed to "read right, then up." In this example the coordinates of Red Hill are 492838E, 4252461N. The full coordinate description must include the UTM zone number found on the map margin.

People who have done a lot of hiking with paper maps swear by the UTM system, claiming it is much easier to measure coordinates from the map. This is undoubtedly true, but UTM has its own limitations. Foremost is that it isn't at all intuitive. If you come across UTM coordinates for an unfamiliar place you won't have any idea where it is, unless you have committed the system to memory. Take a coordinate beginning with 13T, for example. Is it in Nebraska or Arkansas? At least with latitude and longitude, you have some idea what part of the country you're talking about. Another problem is that the UTM grid for each zone is completely separate from all other grids. This becomes a problem when you plan a trek that cuts across more than one zone.

With the coming of electronic maps the advantages of the UTM system are largely past. It's just as easy to read latitude and longitude as UTM from your computer screen. And almost without exception, online and printed GPS waypoint coordinates are published as latitudes and longitudes. If you are in the military or belong to a search-and-rescue team, you'll need to know UTM. And if you intend to do much hiking in the wilderness carrying paper topo maps with you, it might be worth learning. For the rest of us, it's probably not necessary.

Software maps

There are several problems with paper maps. First, each map only covers a limited area, so if your journey takes you any distance you'll have to carry several maps. Second, it's not all that easy to read latitude and longitude coordinates from the map. Nor can you easily determine the exact elevation profile of your planned journey. Will it be a steady climb or filled with hills and dales? After a bit of practice studying paper maps you'll get better at interpreting elevation variations, but it will still take you considerable effort for a hike of any distance. All these problems can be overcome through the use of software maps.

Today, there are many types of software maps. Most are designed to run on Windows PCs, while a few also have Mac versions. Some, like Garmin's *MapSource* (http://www.garmin.com) or Magellan's *MapSend* (http://www.magellangps.com), are designed to load maps directly into compatible GPS receivers. These programs not only let you work from a PC, they also display detailed maps of a region directly on your GPS receiver's screen (albeit on a very small one). Each company uses a proprietary communications protocol that only works with their own receivers.

Other programs are designed to run strictly on a personal computer. They interface to your GPS receiver by way of a serial or USB cable. These programs work with a wide variety of receivers from many manufacturers, but since they require a computer, are not practical to carry in the field. They are best used to plan your route ahead of time. One advantage of software maps is that you can easily print a customized topo map for the specific region of your planned travel.

As with paper maps, software maps fall into two major categories. Planimetric map software is designed for highway navigation. Such programs provide detailed information about roads, freeway exits, and highway mileage. Some can even use voice commands to guide you to exact street addresses. DeLorme's *Street Atlas USA* (http://www.delorme.com) is a well-known example. Garmin's *MapSource Roads & Recreation* and Magellan's *MapSend Streets* also fit into this category. As with paper maps, this type of program is great for getting you to the trailhead but of limited use once you are on the trail.

Topographic map software is much more useful for an actual hike. One type of program starts with scanned versions of USGS topo maps. These are sometimes called raster-graphics maps because of the way the map is digitized. When viewed on the computer screen, the display looks just like a digital version of a paper topo map.

The two most widely-used raster graphics programs are *Topo!* from National Geographic (http://maps.nationalgeographic.com/topo/) and *Terrain Navigator* from Maptech (http://www.maptech.com). Both companies offer seamless map coverage of entire states or major recreation areas at resolutions down to the USGS 7.5-minute

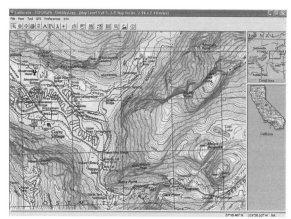

Upper Yosemite Valley as shown by Topo! software. This is typical of the kind of display produced by a raster graphics mapping program. (Image courtesy of National Geographic Topo! software.)

scale, meaning you don't have to struggle to piece together data from separate paper maps. Both also allow you to measure elevation profiles derived from the USGS digital elevation model (DEM) for each map. And both interface to a wide variety of GPS receivers. You can create waypoints and routes in software and automatically upload them to your receiver without having to enter data laboriously via the receiver's clumsy interface. You can also download stored waypoints and tracks from your receiver into the software program so you can see precisely where you have traveled.

Another type of program uses what's known as a vector graphics map. Rather than starting from scanned images of paper maps, it stores the shapes of the terrain contours, roads, and rivers as digital lines. This approach greatly reduces the memory required to store

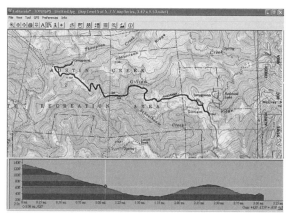

Software maps allow you to see the elevation profile of an intended route. (Image courtesy of National Geographic Topo! software.)

a given geography and makes it easier to provide enhanced graphics such as 3D shading, but you may lose other information typically shown on a USGS map. Man-made features such as buildings and trails could be missing or even misplaced.

Vector graphics programs offer a similar suite of functions as raster-graphics programs. You can create and download waypoints and routes, plot elevation profiles, and transfer data from your GPS receiver into the software program. The efficiency of this type of program is demonstrated by the fact you can purchase vector-based topo software for the whole United States for about the same price as a raster-based program costs for a single state. DeLorme's *TopoUSA* (http://www.delorme.com) is the most popular vector graphics mapping program currently available. Garmin's *MapSource Topo* and Magellan's *MapSend Topo* are two other examples, but these work only with receivers from their respective companies.

If you spend any time browsing Internet newsgroups you'll find strong support for two other programs: *OziExplorer* (http://www.oziexplorer.com/) and *Fugawi* (http://www.fugawi.com). These are both very flexible programs that allow you to work with scanned maps from any source. Load any digitized raster-graphics map into the program, calibrate it by entering the datum and the coordinates of several map locations, and the program does the rest. You can download waypoints and track logs from your GPS receiver to the computer or upload them from the computer to your receiver. Both programs provide a variety of advanced features.

OziExplorer and Fugawi are different from other programs in that they work with virtually any digitized raster-graphics map. With the right maps, they can work worldwide; products such as Terrain Navigator, Topo!, or TopoUSA provide only limited geographical coverage. But this strength is also their weakness. Terrain Navigator, Topo!, and TopoUSA are complete, turnkey systems that include both maps and software interface. Load the program into your computer and you are immediately ready to go. Neither OziExplorer nor Fugawi include maps—you have to obtain them from other sources. There are many on-line sites where you can obtain free or low-cost maps, and if you have access to a scanner you can make your own. If you are technically inclined and comfortable with the Internet, you may find OziExplorer or Fugawi to be the perfect choice. If you just want to get up and running quickly, stick to a turnkey product.

Physical connections and interface protocols

The final thing you'll need to understand about connecting your GPS receiver to a personal computer is the actual physical connection and interface protocol. Most receivers on the market today, including those from Garmin and Magellan, connect to a personal computer by way of a 9-pin serial connection. This connector has historically come standard with almost all new PCs, but an increasing number of newer computers have abandoned it in favor of the much improved and faster USB interface. GPS receiver manufacturers have been slow to address this trend and don't generally offer USB-compatible interfaces. Given the trend among PC manufacturers, this situation will soon have to change. Garmin's GPSMAP 60C and 60CS are the first consumer receivers to make this important step forward. Owners of older GPS receivers who have upgraded to a new computer sans serial interface will either have to install a third-party serial card or try to use an external USB-to-serial adapter from a supplier such as Belkin (http://www.belkin.com). Before trying this latter approach, though, check with the manufacturer of your GPS receiver. The track record of success for such adapters has been somewhat sporadic, and you may be able to get advice on what brands or configurations have been most successful with your particular receiver.

Even after you've made a good physical connection between the GPS receiver and the computer, you still need to make sure the two are speaking the same software language. It's the equivalent of two people having a conversation in which one person is speaking French and the other English. Unless they both understand both languages, the conversation will be very difficult.

The industry-standard for communicating between GPS receiver and computer is known as NMEA 0183. Developed by the National Marine Electronics Association (http://www.nmea.org), it defines the formats for messages between the two units. The current version of the standard is 3.01, issued in January of 2002, but your receiver and mapping software should support older versions as well, specifically versions 1.5, 2.1, or 2.3. Both Magellan and Garmin support versions of this standard. Garmin also provides additional proprietary capability, not surprisingly called the GARMIN interface protocol. It is supported by most third-party software programs and in most software, it is the preferred interface for use with GARMIN receivers.

8
Route Planning and Navigation

TO GET THE MOST BENEFIT from your GPS receiver, you need to know how to use it to navigate routes that include intermediate destinations along the way. It's the equivalent of going out for an afternoon of errands: you plan to stop at the post office to buy some stamps, then on to the hardware store and the gym before finishing up at the grocery store and returning home. If you've lived in the area for awhile you can make the trip by memory. But what if you're new in town? You'll probably want to check a map and plan your itinerary. You wouldn't want to go to the grocery store first, leaving your ice cream to melt while you get in a workout at the gym!

GPS routes

A GPS *route* is a similar concept. You first enter a series of waypoints, then tell your receiver the sequence you want to go to them. When you activate the route function your receiver automatically guides you to the first destination just as if you had used the GOTO function. When you get there it automatically switches to guide you to the next waypoint. It continues for each waypoint in succession until you arrive at your final destination.

Think of a route as a series of GOTO functions programmed to occur one after the other. There's nothing you can do with a route you couldn't also do by manually using the GOTO function. The advantage of the ROUTE function is that it automates the navigation process. You don't need to memorize the names of a dozen or more waypoints and the order you want to reach them. You can also use a route over again without having to check your notes or remember waypoint lists. And most receivers allow you to reverse a route so you can easily get back to where you started.

Open-loop route (left) and closed-loop route (right).

The important thing is to understand what a route is and how to
follow it. It's not absolutely necessary to know how to use the actual
ROUTE function in your receiver—some expert navigators never use
anything more than the GOTO function—but if you intend to do any
serious wilderness navigation it is critical you at least understand
how to construct and follow a multi-leg route. And if you know this,
you might as well learn how to use the route function.

There are two kinds of routes: open-loop and closed loop. An open-
loop route is one that goes from a starting point to a destination,
traveling through intermediate points along the way. To get back to
the starting point, you follow the route in reverse, a technique known
as *reversing* the route.

A closed-loop route goes from a starting point through a series
of intermediate destinations and ends up back at the starting point
without reversing. The afternoon of errands we described at the
beginning of the chapter is an example of a closed-loop route—you
don't need to return via the hardware store and post office just to get
back home.

Your GPS receiver can handle either type of route interchangeably.
In fact, it doesn't even know or care whether the route is open loop
or closed loop. It just knows to guide you to a series of waypoints in
the order you have told it. It's only important for *you* to know if it is
an open-loop route so you can be sure you remember how to reverse
the route when you reach the end.

An example of an open loop route is the trail to the top of Half
Dome in Yosemite National Park. We will use this as our example for
programming a route into your receiver.

First, let's review the route as shown on the map. Starting at the
Happy Isles trailhead, follow the Mist Trail to the top of Vernal Fall,
then continue on to the top of Nevada Fall. There, join the John Muir

Trail to its intersection with the Half Dome Trail. Turn north, taking the Half Dome Trail all the way to the peak. You don't want to
get confused by various other trails that enter and depart along the
way, so you can define a "route" consisting of the trails and the key
intersections along the way. Of course you will eventually want to get
back to where you started, but you can do this simply by reversing
the route. So your "route" only needs to define the first half of the
journey.

Planning a route with paper maps

Let's first see how to plan the route using USGS 7.5-minute paper
maps. The maps you want are "Half Dome, CA" and "Yosemite Falls,
CA." Immediately you discover the first problem with paper maps.
All but a very small part of the trail is on the Half Dome map, but you
need both maps to see your entire route. The part missing from Half
Dome is so small you'd probably not carry the Yosemite Falls map
on your hike, but you still need it during the planning process so you

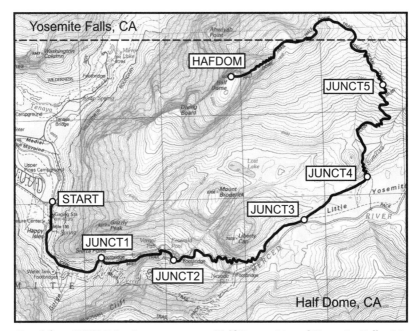

*Detail from USGS 7.5-minute topo maps Half Dome, CA and Yosemite Falls, CA,
showing the trail to Half Dome and possible waypoint locations and names. The
dashed line indicates the transition between the two maps.*

can at least be familiar with that part of the trail. (You might even want to cut and paste the small portion of the Yosemite Falls map onto the Half Dome map you carry on the hike.)

First trace out your route on the map using a pencil or highlighter pen. Then look for the important trail junctions and other points of interest—anything that will help you stay on the right path or lead you to something you want to see. These are the locations you will program into your receiver as GPS waypoints.

The example map shows seven waypoints, including the starting and ending points. This amounts to a waypoint roughly every mile, which is a reasonable interval. Of course you should pick waypoints based on how they will help you navigate rather than simply choosing a fixed interval between them. The example waypoints represent trail junctions where there's some risk you might make a wrong turn.

For each waypoint draw a crosshair centered on it. This makes it easier to accurately read latitude and longitude. Then give the waypoint a name. Since you will program this name into your GPS receiver, make sure it fits within the receiver's naming limitations. Some receivers only accept waypoint names up to six characters long; others accept 12 or more characters. Even if they do, shorter names are usually better, especially when using a mapping receiver. You don't want the small map display cluttered with long waypoint names.

Reading waypoint coordinates

Now comes the challenging part: determining the waypoint coordinates. For this example we'll see how to measure latitude and longitude, although you could also easily use UTM; the 1997 edition of Half Dome has a full UTM grid printed on it.

To read latitude and longitude you need a special latitude-longitude ruler. You can get nice plastic ones at an outdoor specialty shop or you can photocopy the one on Page 112. Before using it you need to prepare the map by drawing ruled lines at the 2.5 minute points. Look for the 2.5-minute tic marks along the map neatlines. (There are also crosshairs within the map where these latitude and longitude lines intersect.) Lay down a yardstick and carefully draw lines to connect the corresponding marks on each side of the map. For longitude, extend the lines all the way to the edge of the paper. Do this for both the interior 2.5-minute lines and the longitude neatlines. (For latitude, you don't need to extend the lines beyond the neatlines.) When finished, your map should look similar to the illustration.

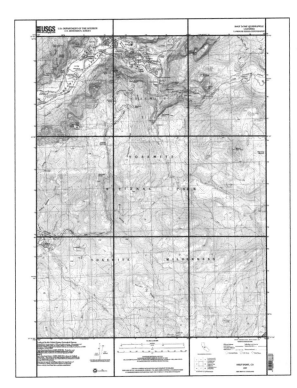

USGS 7.5-minute map Half Dome, CA, showing ruled lines necessary to read latitude and longitude.

Reading latitude is fairly simple. Align the ends of the latitude scale with the 2.5-minute lines on either side of the point you want to measure, making sure the north end of the scale is oriented toward the top of the map. Reading upward from the bottom, the scale shows the *incremental* latitude in minutes and seconds you must add to the absolute latitude of the lower 2.5-minute line. If your waypoint doesn't align exactly with a line on the ruler, try to estimate its position to the nearest tenth of a second.

Notice the scale has two sets of numbers, one beginning with 0 and one beginning with 30. Which set you use depends on the latitude of the lower 2.5-minute line. If it is on an even minute of latitude, use the scale beginning with 0. If it is on a 30-second increment, use the scale beginning with 30.

Reading longitude is only slightly more complicated. Remember that the distance between lines of longitude decreases as you move away from the equator, so it's not possible to construct a fixed-length scale that's right for all maps. But there's still a way. Just tilt the ruler

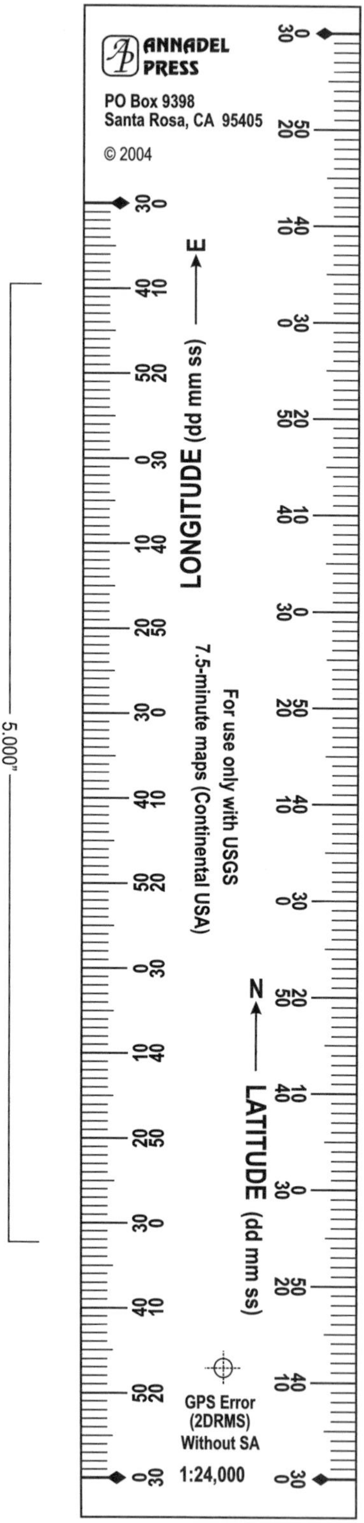

ANNADEL PRESS

PO Box 9398
Santa Rosa, CA 95405

© 2004

E

LONGITUDE (dd mm ss)

7.5-minute maps (Continental USA)

For use only with USGS

5.000"

N

LATITUDE (dd mm ss)

GPS Error
(2DRMS)
Without SA

1:24,000

A latitude-longitude ruler enables you to read coordinates from a topo map. The one shown here is designed for USGS 7.5-minute maps. You may photocopy it for your own personal use. Read the text for instructions on its use.

You can purchase more sophisticated rulers with markings for many different map scales from a good outdoor specialty shop.

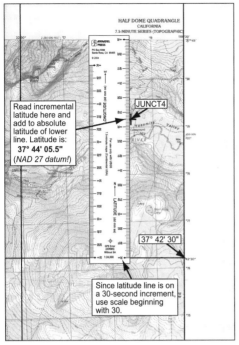

Read incremental latitude here and add to absolute latitude of lower line. Latitude is: **37° 44' 05.5"** (*NAD 27 datum!*)

JUNCT4

37° 42' 30"

Since latitude line is on a 30-second increment, use scale beginning with 30.

Read latitude by orienting the ruler so the latitude scale aligns with the 2.5-minute lines. Orient the scale so the NORTH indicator points up. Add the incremental latitude of the ruler to the absolute latitude of the lower line. In this example, the lower line is on a 30-second increment, so you use the scale beginning with 30.

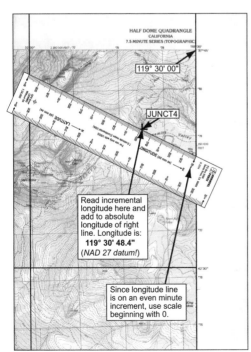

119° 30' 00"

JUNCT4

Read incremental longitude here and add to absolute longitude of right line. Longitude is: **119° 30' 48.4"** (*NAD 27 datum!*)

Since longitude line is on an even minute increment, use scale beginning with 0.

Read longitude by tilting the ruler so the ends of the longitude scale align with the ruled 2.5-minute longitude lines. Be sure to orient the scale so the EAST indicator points to the right. Add the incremental longitude of the ruler to the absolute longitude of the right line. In this example, the right line is on an even minute of longitude, so you use the scale beginning with 0.

as shown in the illustration until both ends align with the 2.5 minute longitude lines, making sure the east end of the scale is on the right. Keeping the scale at this angle, slide it up or down until you can read the longitude of the point of interest. Repeat this process for all the rest of the waypoints you have identified.

Remember to check the map's datum before entering the coordinates into your GPS receiver. Most USGS maps, including this one of Half Dome, still use NAD 27, and you'll need to set this datum in your receiver before entering the coordinates.

Creating the route

Once you've measured all the waypoints you're ready to create the route. First enter the coordinates of each waypoint, making sure the map datum and position format are set properly (in this example, they are NAD 27 and degrees-minutes-seconds). Now you're ready to create the route.

The details of how to do this are different depending on your receiver, so you'll need to read your instruction manual for specific details. In general, the sequence goes something like this:

1. Select the ROUTE page on your receiver
2. Select "NEW" or an unused route on the screen
3. In the first waypoint position, enter the name of the starting waypoint for the route
4. Continue entering waypoints in subsequent positions in the order you want to go to them
5. Name the route and save it in memory

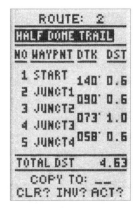

Once a route has been entered and saved, you can use it for navigation. Again, check your instruction manual for details. Typically, you go to the ROUTE page, choose the route you want, and select the key labeled something like "NAVIGATE," "FOLLOW," or "ACTIVATE."

Remember the first waypoint in the route is considered the starting point. So when you activate a route, it immediately directs

Route screen on the Garmin GPS 12 XL. As with all receivers, the indicated straight-line distances between waypoints are signifcantly shorter than the true hiking distances.

you to the second waypoint, even if you are nowhere near the starting point. You might wonder why you even need to enter the starting point, but just remember it becomes very important if you plan to use the route reversal feature to lead you back to the beginning.

Planning a route with software maps

Route planning with paper maps is tedious, especially when it comes to reading waypoint coordinates. Software maps make the process much easier. You can easily draw your intended route onto the map, read its total length, and generate an elevation profile. You can quickly place waypoints on the route and electronically transfer their coordinates to your GPS receiver. Once you have used software maps you'll find it difficult to ever go back to using paper maps!

Let's take a quick look at how you would plan the same route to the top of Half Dome Using a software map. For our example we will use National Geographic's *Topo!* state-series software for California, but the process is similar for other software packages.

After installing the software on your PC, launch the program and zoom in on the area around Half Dome. With *Topo!*, the highest zoom

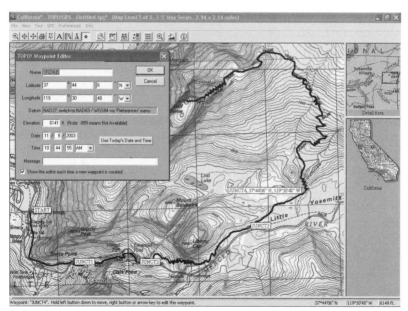

Software maps make it easy to create waypoints and load them into your GPS receiver. This is the waypoint screen from National Geographic's TOPO! software. (Image courtesy of National Geographic Topo! software.)

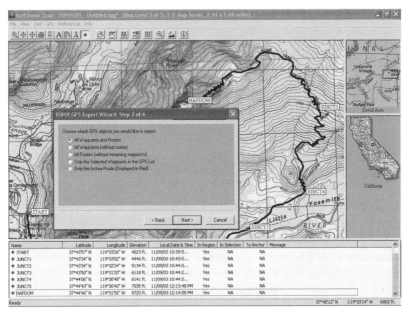

After creating a list of waypoints it can easily be uploaded to a GPS receiver. (Image courtesy of National Geographic Topo! software.)

level displays USGS 7.5-minute maps. The first difference you'll notice is its seamless coverage. You'll hardly even be aware that the trail stretches across two paper maps.

Next, use the Route tool to draw your intended route on the display. It takes a little practice to draw an accurate trail using *Topo!'s* tool. You'll probably need to use the right mouse button to erase mistakes several times along the way. But with care, you'll eventually end up with a reasonable representation of the route. At this point you can, if you choose, get a readout of trail length or elevation profile.

Now you're ready to add waypoints using the Waypoint tool. Click the pointer on each location and a dialog box comes up giving you the location and other information. Highlight the name box and type in the new name. Click "OK" and the waypoint shows up on the screen. Do this for each waypoint you want to add. When finished, you'll have a list of waypoints ready to be loaded into your GPS receiver. Connect your receiver to your computer using the appropriate cable and select the GPS menu to upload the information—much simpler and more foolproof than using paper maps!

PART 4:
Recovering from Disaster

Key Concepts in Part 4

· Essential items for wilderness travel
· Planning ahead to avoid disaster
· Basic map and compass skills
· Wilderness navigation without GPS
· Advantages of waiting for rescue vs. finding your own way out
· Primitive methods for finding your way without map or compass

9
Preparing for Disaster

THE CHAPTERS IN THIS SECTION deal with the inevitable question: "What do I do when I'm out in the wilderness and my GPS receiver fails?" First, let me point out this is not a book on outdoor survival. If you intend to spend much time in the wilderness, you should know many survival techniques that we won't cover here. Check the references in the Appendix for information on wilderness survival. What we will cover in this section are alternate navigation techniques—methods you can use to get back to safety if you unexpectedly find yourself without a working GPS receiver.

Essential items

The best way to deal with disaster is to avoid it occurring in the first place. It doesn't take a lot of preparation to turn what could have been a serious incident into something that's little more than a momentary inconvenience. Harvey Manning, in the classic *Backpacking One Step at a Time*, describes what he calls the "Ten Essentials," originally compiled by the Mountaineers back in the 1930s for use by climbers. Updated for today's needs, it is a good list for anyone intending to travel more than an hour or two from civilization. Everything here should fit in an ordinary daypack with room to spare:

1. **Extra Clothing.** Even if you only plan to go out for a day hike, take a few key items of clothing. You primarily need to protect against unexpectedly cool and windy weather, and perhaps the occasional rain shower. Check the weather forecast for the next several days and pack the minimum you think you would need if you were stuck overnight. A windproof jacket is essential. Don't expect an ordinary fleece jacket to protect you in even moderate winds without a windproof shell. If rain is even remotely possible, your jacket

The Ten Essentials of Wilderness Exploration

1. Extra clothing
2. Extra food and water
3. Sunglasses
4. Knife
5. Fire starter
6. Matches
7. First-aid kit
8. Flashlight
9. Map and pen/pencil
10. Compass

should be waterproof. Be wary of inexpensive nylon clothing advertised as "water resistant." Such material isn't designed to keep you dry for extended periods. "Waterproof breathable" fabric is more expensive but well worth it if you're caught in a downpour.

Long pants and a wide-brimmed hat are also important. Cargo pants with zip-off legs let you easily adapt to changing weather conditions without adding much bulk in a daypack. Other recommended items are an extra pair of socks (in case you get wet crossing a stream) and gloves to help keep you warm if you get delayed overnight. Finally, you should always have an aluminum-coated mylar "space blanket" stowed for an emergency. It weighs next to nothing and can keep you remarkably warm if necessary.

2. **Extra Food and Water.** You don't need to pack four-course meals if you're only planning to be out for the morning, but you should always have extra rations to tide you over in an emergency. Energy bars, beef jerky, and freeze-dried backpacker meals (if you have water and a way to heat it) are good alternatives. These rations should be in addition to any food already part of your planned itinerary. Plan so that if nothing goes wrong, you'll still have food left at the end of your journey.

Carry plenty of water, even in regions where ground water is readily available. These days there is almost no natural source you should drink without purifying, so you might want to carry water purification tablets or a water filter. When purchasing a filter, look for one rated to 0.2 microns that will not only screen out giardia, the most common problem, but also other harmful bacteria. Note that water filters won't kill viruses unless they also include an iodine treatment—not usually a problem in the US but a definite concern in the third world. Water purification tablets do kill viruses but leave a distinctive chemical taste. Tablets don't have an indefinite shelf life and deteriorate quickly after the bottle is opened. Follow the instructions on the bottle to understand proper use.

3. **Sunglasses.** When this list was originally developed in the 1930s, sunglasses were a relative rarity. Now they are routine. Admittedly they aren't essential in every case, but if you expect to travel over sand, snow, or water, they are required to prevent temporary or permanent eye damage from reflected sunlight. Make sure they are rated to block 100% of both UVA and UVB rays.

4. **Knife.** The Swiss Army knife has been the tried-and-true staple for many years. It's still a good choice, but these days many people have come to prefer a multipurpose tool that includes pliers, scissors, screwdrivers, and numerous other implements in addition to the basic knife. Models by Leatherman (http://www.leatherman. com) and Gerber (http://www.gerbertools.com) are well-designed, reliable, and priced to match.

5. **Fire Starter.** Even in wooded areas, it might not be that easy to start a fire in an emergency. You don't want to waste all your matches trying to light damp leaves or green pine needles. Solid fuel tablets or jellied fuel tubes, available at camping supply stores, can get a roaring fire started with just one match. Even a simple candle can be better than nothing.

6. **Matches.** Although you may take a good supply of ordinary matches, make sure you supplement those with specialty waterproof matches. You might also consider packing a butane pocket lighter. Everyone in your group except small children should carry their own supply of matches.

7. **First-aid kit.** A minimum first-aid kit should include adhesive bandages and a few larger gauze pads, aspirin or ibuprofen, adhesive tape, antibacterial ointment, a good pair of tweezers, and a first-aid instruction manual. For larger groups or extended trips, the kit should necessarily be larger and more extensive. One generally useful item is a 25-foot length of braided nylon or parachute cord. Check your local outdoor specialty shop for pre-assembled kits or study their contents to aid in assembling your own.

8. **Flashlight.** As with matches, everyone in a group should carry at least a small flashlight. Those by Mag-Lite (http://www.maglite.com) are durable and reliable. You may also want to check out some of the newer LED-based flashlights that put out bright illumination with less drain on batteries than incandescent lights. Headlamps have also become more popular in recent times, as they allow you to keep both hands free for other activities.

9/10. **Map and Compass.** As we have already described, map and compass are essential any time you venture into the wilderness. You'll want a pen or pencil to make notations on the map.

Of course if you only intend to travel through the local park, a survival kit this extensive is hardly necessary. But the subject of this section is recovering from disaster; if you drop and break your GPS receiver in the local park, it might be a disaster to your pocketbook but hardly something that will keep you from finding your way home. For the kinds of wilderness travels implied in these chapters, every one of these essentials should be in your pack.

GPS survival kit

The GPS navigator needs to expand on this list slightly by adding three additional things:

> GPS receiver
> Sturdy carrying case
> Extra batteries

REMEMBER: your GPS receiver does not replace the map and compass, it is in *addition* to them. You still need the map and compass so you can navigate if your GPS receiver fails. In the next chapter we'll see how to do this.

It's important to keep your receiver in a carrying case when it is not being used. A GPS receiver is not indestructible, and letting it bang around loosely in your pack or pocket will only hasten its demise. On some receivers, the connections between the LCD display and the internal electronics are particularly susceptible. If you start noticing lines running horizontally or vertically through the display you'll know the connections are suspect. Sometimes you can temporarily solve the problem by striking the receiver against the palm of your hand (never anything harder), but only try this as a last resort.

The carrying case can be one originally designed for a digital camera or one custom-designed for your receiver. The important thing is that it be sufficiently padded to provide reasonable protection.

Extra batteries are an absolute necessity. Stick a few extra AA cells in your pocket or backpack, or in the side pocket of your receiver's case, if it has one. You'll have cheap, lightweight insurance against unexpected power loss. Not having spare batteries in the wilderness should be a criminal offense.

These backup batteries should be alkaline, not NiCad or LiMH rechargeables. Alkalines will not only keep your receiver operating longer (over twice as many hours as NiCad), they also have considerably longer shelf life. NiCad and LiMH rechargeables will slowly discharge just sitting on the shelf, and after only a few weeks will need to be recharged. Rechargable batteries are fine for casual use on day-hikes where you have easy access to a charger, but don't rely on them in the wilderness. For cold-weather use, you might even want to consider lithium batteries. Although much more expensive than alkalines, their cold-weather performance is considerably better. See Page 180 or check your GPS receiver's instruction manual for more information on battery compatibility.

Other Backup Plans

Spare GPS Receiver. Aircraft, ships, and spacecraft all have double or triple redundant navigation systems. When your life depends on it, you can't allow yourself to be put in jeopardy by a single instrument failure. The serious outdoor navigator would do well to consider the same possibility and invest in a second GPS receiver as a back-up.

This recommendation isn't intended to stimulate the economy by helping sell GPS receivers. If your safety doesn't depend on your GPS receiver, if you can find your way home without it, you probably don't need to make the investment. But if you plan a journey into serious wilderness—the wilds of Alaska or Canada, for example—ask yourself just how important it is that you have a working GPS receiver. Spending an extra $100 on a backup receiver may be a minor additional expense compared to the total cost of your trip.

Lightweight models such as the Garmin Geko make it difficult to claim you can't afford the extra weight. Just be sure that if you bring a second receiver you know how to use it. You don't want to be struggling to learn a new receiver at what is already a time of serious stress. This is one argument in favor of selecting a back-up receiver from the same family as your primary receiver. It might not have all the same features, but at least it will have a familiar interface.

There are a couple of other things to remember when bringing a back-up receiver. First, make sure it, too, has fresh batteries, and that you have appropriate spares. The Geko, for example, uses AAA batteries. Your primary receiver probably uses AA cells. So you would need to bring some of each.

Second, remember to turn on your backup receiver and mark your position at the beginning of the journey. It's best if you enter all the intermediate waypoints as well. If you get into a situation where you need to depend on a back-up receiver to aid your return, you want to make sure it knows where you're going.

If there is more than one person in your party, spread the GPS receivers out among them. That way, if you get separated or someone loses a backpack over a cliff or down a river, you haven't also automatically lost your back-up.

Cell Phone. Another survival item you might be considering is a cellular telephone. In movies and television ads, such phones always work with crystal clarity. In the wilderness, though, they probably won't. Telephone companies are understandably driven by profit, so they install base stations in locations they know will get used. Wilderness areas aren't at the top of their coverage list.

Unless you know you are going to be within range of a cellular base station, you shouldn't depend on a cell phone to get you out of a fix. You might still want to bring it along, and you may be pleasantly surprised. In the California desert I've gotten good reception 50 miles from the nearest habitation and well away from the coverage limits shown on the telephone company's maps. But I always regard such a result as a lucky happenstance and would never trust my safety to achieving a repeat performance.

Finally, any time you plan a journey into the wilderness, even if just for a few hours, you should let someone know your plan and when you intend to return. You never know when an accident might interrupt your travel. If you suddenly find yourself with a serious injury, you might not be able to get back even if your GPS receiver is still working. If you don't return in a timely manner, there will at least be someone who can initiate a search-and-rescue operation.

10
Map and Compass Navigation

S O FAR, MAPS AND COMPASSES have played only supporting roles in outdoor navigation. As long as you have a working GPS receiver with all necessary waypoints stored properly, you can safely use it as your primary navigation tool. But what do you do if your receiver fails? Perhaps the batteries died and you don't have spares. Or maybe it took a hard blow in a fall, breaking the display? Or even worse, maybe you lost it in a lake or over a precipitous chasm? Now what? How do you get back to safety?

In this chapter we'll assume you've done the sensible thing and brought along a topo map and compass. We'll also assume it's not as simple as following a well-marked trail back to your starting point. Perhaps it's been snowing and your tracks are covered. Maybe you've done serious cross-country hiking or spent the day canoeing on a remote, unfamiliar lake. You need to get back using only your map, compass, and navigation skills. This chapter won't teach you everything about map and compass navigation—for that, pick up a good guide like the Sierra Club's *Land Navigation Handbook* by W. S. Kals—but you'll learn enough to get by in an emergency.

First, remember to stay calm. You've sensibly packed a map and compass, so you're already halfway home. Now you just need relax and remember how to use them. With a map and compass, getting back to safety involves four steps:

1. Determine your present position
2. Decide on your destination
3. Identify the best route to get there
4. Follow the chosen route, making adjustments as necessary along the way

Determining your present position

Before you can figure out how to get to safety, you first have to know where you are. Don't panic and start heading in a random direction, or in what you think might be the right direction without confirming it. Take the time to really identify where you are.

One fundamental skill you should make a habit is to regularly correlate your GPS position with the map. That way if the receiver fails you already have a good idea of your location. Unfortunately, too many people fail to do this. How do you find your position when you haven't been keeping careful track? We will describe three ways: triangulation, dead reckoning, and altimeter navigation. But none of these are as good as correlating your position as you travel.

Triangulation

The easiest approach, if the opportunity presents itself, is to triangulate your position from objects you can see in the landscape. It's similar to how your GPS receiver works, but of course you're not using satellites, you must use identifiable objects in the landscape.

Orienting the map. You first need to orient your map to the surroundings. When you're facing north you want the top of the map to also be facing north. That way it's easy to match a feature in the distance to its corresponding feature on the map.

Do this by using your compass. Set it to an indicated *true* bearing of 0° and lay it pointing north on the map so the side of the compass

To orient your map to the surroundings, set the bearing indicator to 0° true and align the edge of the compass with the neatline of the map. Rotate map and compass together to box the magnetic needle inside the north reference indicator. Note this compass has been adjusted to compensate for magnetic declination.

aligns with a map border (neatline) as shown in the photo.

Now rotate map and compass together until the magnetic needle is boxed inside the north reference indicator. Your map is now aligned to the landscape.

This only works with a compass that's been set to compensate for local declination. Otherwise you need to make the adjustment by mentally correcting for declination—not something you should have to worry about when you're already stressed from having just lost your primary navigation tool. This is where you will really appreciate a compass with adjustable declination. It's bad enough that you're lost, you don't want to further complicate things by forgetting whether you are supposed to add or subtract declination to your compass readings. (If you ignore this advice and choose to navigate by magnetic bearings, now would be a good time to brush up on the principles of declination correction described on Page 59.)

Triangulating your position. Now that you've got the map properly oriented, you're ready to triangulate your position. Here's how:

1. Identify at least two objects (preferably three) in your field of view that are also on the map. These can be prominent mountain peaks, radio towers, waterfalls, or just about anything else you can *reliably* identify in both your surroundings and on the map. Ideally, the objects should be at close to right angles from each other, though this is not always possible. Avoid objects that are in line or 180° apart.

    If you happen to be on a known river, trail, ridge line, gully or similar geographic feature you only need to identify one additional object (preferably two). Such features are known as *handrails*, and you can use them to help identify your position.

    If you can't spot suitable objects from your current position, do a little reconnaissance. Climb to the top of a nearby hill—if you can do it safely—or move to an area with a better view: a meadow or forest clearing, for example. Be cautious when moving, and don't lose visual contact with others in your party.

2. Use your compass to read the bearing to each object. You will be plotting these bearings on the map, so they need to be referenced to true north. Again I'll recommend you invest in a compass with adjustable declination and get comfortable using it.

    Take care to get your compass readings as accurate as possible.

It's a little easier with a mirror compass, as you can view both the object and the compass vial at the same time. With a simple base-plate compass, you'll have to point it carefully at the object before rotating the vial. Be sure to keep the compass level so the magnetic needle rotates freely.

As shown in the diagram, the uncertainty in your position increases the farther you are from the reference object. If you can only measure an object's bearing to within 5°, the uncertainty in your position will be 450 feet per mile. If the object is a mountain peak 10 miles away, your uncertainty is 4500 feet—nearly a mile! By improving the accuracy of your measurements to 2° the uncertainty drops to only 180 feet per mile—a good reason to measure bearings as accurately as possible!

With two people, you can improve the accuracy of measurements taken with a simple baseplate compass. One person kneels down, holds the compass at eye level (keeping it level), and points it at the object. The other person remains standing to view the compass vial. This person carefully rotates the vial to center the compass needle inside the north reference indicator while the

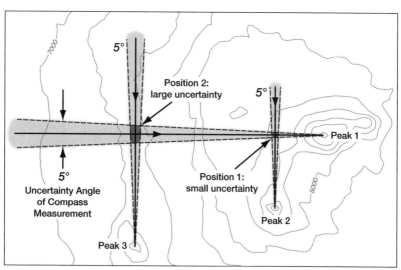

When triangulating your position, the farther you are from the reference ob-jects, the greater the uncertainty in your position. This example assumes you can measure an object's bearing to an accuracy of 5°. At Position 1, you are close to the reference objects and the uncertainty is small. At Position 2, the un-certainty is larger, especially because you are far from Peak 1.

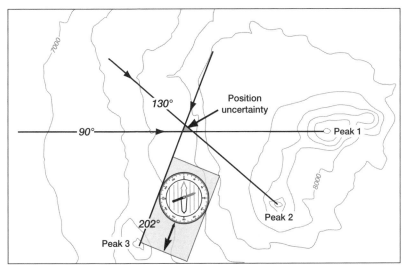

To triangulate your position, plot the bearings you have measured from your current position to at least two (preferably three) objects you have identified on the map. Notice that with three objects, the lines probably won't all intersect at the same spot. You are most likely somewhere within the triangle of uncertainty.

kneeling person keeps the compass level and pointed at the object.

3. Correct the measured bearings for magnetic declination, if necessary.

4. For each object, draw a line on the map through the object at the bearing angle you measured to it. This line is known as a *position line*. You know that you must be somewhere along this line.

In this situation, the bearings you measured are from your unknown position to the known object. This is opposite of the situation described in Chapter 3, where you knew your current position but not your destination. Here, after setting the correct bearing on the vial, lay the compass on the map so the direction-of-travel arrow points in the direction of the object. The front edge of the compass should be touching it as shown in the illustration. Now adjust the entire compass (don't turn the vial!) so that 0 degrees points to the top of the map while the front edge of the compass remains in contact with the object. (Don't worry about where the magnetic needle points.) Some compasses include north-south orienting lines to make this job a little easier.

Using a pencil, draw a line along the edge of the compass from

To read the bearing of an object with a mirror compass, aim the notch on top of the lid at the object so the line down the center of the mirror runs through the apparent center of the vial. Rotate the vial while watching it in the mirror until the north reference indicator aligns with the magnetic needle.

the known object toward your location. If the distance is farther than the length of the compass, use a straightedge to extend it. In the unlikely event you've brought along a ruler for this purpose, that's great. Otherwise, find something else long and straight—the edge of a book or map, for instance. You can also make your own straightedge by folding a sheet of paper in half or tightly stretching a piece of string or fishing line.

5. If you took bearings to two or more objects, your position is where the lines intersect. If you took only one bearing and used a known feature like a river as a handrail, your position is where the bearing line intersects the river.

Triangulation is a reasonably accurate way to find your position, though it's not perfect. You'll quickly discover this if you take bearings to more than two objects and plot all the position lines on the map. It's unlikely they'll all intersect at the same spot, but if you've made careful measurements they should be close. The distance between the various intersections is a good approximation of the error in your measurements.

Dead reckoning

Suppose you can't spot any identifiable features in the landscape—there's nothing but forest or unbroken swampland, for instance, or perhaps it's foggy. Now it becomes more of a challenge. Your objective becomes one of navigating in the correct general direction until you can get to a more identifiable area. This is known by mariners as *dead reckoning* (where "dead" doesn't necessarily reflect on the fate of its user, but rather is short for "deduced").

Here is where you need to stop and think. You should know where on the map you started from, and you will usually have a general idea of which direction you have been traveling. You should also have some idea of how long you have been out. If you can estimate how far you have traveled and what direction you have been moving, you can get a rough idea of where you are from your starting point.

Estimating the distance traveled. Your first task is to estimate the distance you have traveled. If you have been hiking, you can apply some general guidelines (for other modes of transportation you'll have to make your own estimates). I'll caution you that it's always risky to publish such guidelines, because every situation is different. A young athlete with only a water bottle will move significantly faster than a 50-year old office manager carrying a 40-pound pack.

With that caution in mind, here is a very simplified two-step approach. You first need to estimate your average speed. Then you need to estimate how long you have been traveling. Knowing these two things, you can estimate distance you have covered.

In this simplified approach we assume you can travel at a standard speed on level ground. Then we adjust that rate to account for terrain that is climbing or descending, and make a further adjustment to account for the type of terrain. This simplified approach does not take into account fatigue, you'll have to account for that on your own.

The following guidelines provide a starting point for estimating walking speeds. The results agree to within 10% of a somewhat different formula published by Kals in *Land Navigation Handbook.* (Don't hesitate to modify the numbers to account for your own hiking style.)

- On level ground and average terrain, figure you can walk about 2 miles per hour when carrying a moderate pack up to about 30 lbs.
- For every 200 feet per mile of elevation gain, deduct 0.3 miles per hour
- For every 200 feet per mile of elevation drop, deduct 0.1 miles per hour
- When walking over soft sand or loose rock, cut the calculated speed in half.

These guidelines apply for elevation gains or losses up to about 800 feet per mile (17% grade). Beyond that, you're on your own.

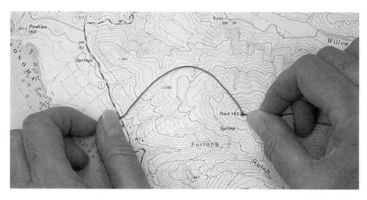

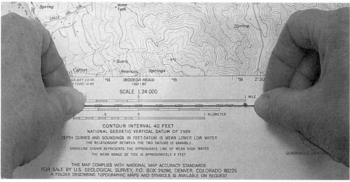

To determine the change in elevation per mile, calculate the total elevation difference and divide by the total distance traveled. You can measure distance by laying a string along your approximate path, then calibrating it against the map scale. A knot at one end of the string makes the measurement easier. In this example the total elevation change is 800 feet and the total distance is 1.5 miles, so the climb is about 500 feet per mile.

Let's look at an example. Suppose you are hiking a trail that climbs 400 feet in one mile. Your approximate speed is therefore 2 mph minus 0.3×2, or 1.4 mph. If your journey was over soft sand, cut the number in half, to 0.7 mph. Of course these are only generalizations—"your mileage may vary." You should do a few hikes in controlled conditions to calibrate your normal speed.

Estimating elevation change. You now know how to estimate your speed, but how do you determine the amount of elevation gain or loss? The easiest way is to use your topo map and a piece of string. You first need to to calibrate the string using the scale at the bottom of the map. Stretch the string between your thumbs so they are exactly a scale mile apart. Then, holding the string tightly, arrange it so it aligns with your route. Read the elevation contours at your starting and ending points. The difference is the elevation gain or loss in one mile. If you've traveled more than a mile, divide the total elevation change by the total distance, or take several one-mile-long readings along your path and use the average.

Estimating your location. Now you have an estimate of your speed and how long you have been hiking. Multiply your speed by your travel time to get the distance traveled. Here's an example. You've been out for six hours. You estimate you've been climbing at a rate of 400 feet per mile over average terrain, so your hiking speed has been 1.4 mph. Multiply 1.4 mph by 6 hours to get a total distance of 8.4 miles. You'd probably want to reduce that a bit to account for fatigue and the occasional rest stop you took along the way.

Finally, draw a line on the map from your starting point in the general direction you estimate you've been heading. You are most likely somewhere along this line. If you had been hiking in a straight line the entire time you would be about 7 to 8 miles away, but that's not usually the case. Here is where you have to apply some judgement and estimate how your actual course came into play. Again, you can use a string that you've calibrated to be about 8 scale miles long. Arrange it in what you believe to roughly approximate your true course to get an idea of where you are.

Altimeter navigation

Before the advent of GPS, navigation by barometric altimeter was a fairly well known, though infrequently used, back-up method. These days you don't hear too much about it. But you can still use it to advantage—if you remembered to pack a barometric altimeter. I'm not talking about the one you might have in your fancy, high-end GPS receiver. If its batteries have run down or you've lost it over a cliff, its internal altimeter will be no more useful to you than its GPS functions. For this approach to work you need a separate, back-up altimeter.

Altimeters come in two varieties: mechanical units with analog dials and electronic units with digital displays. Thommen (www.thommenag.com) is an example of a manufacturer of precision analog altimeters. Brunton (www.brunton.com) makes a fine digital unit, the Sherpa, that also doubles as a wind speed indicator and thermometer. You can also find reasonably good digital altimeters on some high-end watches designed for outdoor adventurers. Digital units usually provide higher resolution readouts, often calibrated to display differences of only a few feet. Analog units generally are calibrated in 20 to 100 foot increments, although you can do a pretty good job of eyeballing intermediate values. Remember there is a difference between readout *resolution* and true *accuracy*. Given that you won't usually be able to calibrate your altimeter to better than 20-foot accuracy anyway, the resolution of a good mechanical unit is more than adequate.

Before you start using a barometric altimeter, you need to understand a little about how it works. As its name implies, it doesn't directly measure true elevation, but rather barometric pressure. Since barometric pressure decreases in a predictable way as you gain elevation, it is possible for the altimeter to give a readout of elevation.

As is usually the case with such matters, it isn't as simple as it first sounds. Barometric pressure is not constant, but changes depending on the weather—the very reason a barometer is useful as a weather forecasting tool. Before you can take accurate elevation readings you first have to perform a calibration. You do this by going to a known elevation and adjusting your altimeter to read that elevation. This can be a trailhead, visitors center, or any other location where the elevation is either posted or can be determined from your topo map. The closer you are to the elevations you plan to hike, the better. Avoid calibrating your altimeter at sea level when you plan to be hiking at 8,000 feet.

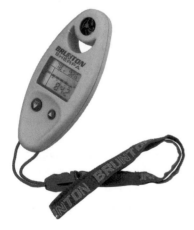

The Brunton Sherpa is a combination instrument that can measure altitude, barometric pressure, temperature, and wind speed. (Brunton)

Over the course of a day, barometric pressure will change with the weather, causing your apparent elevation to change even if you are standing still. But the effect is less than you might think. According to W. S. Kals in the classic *Land Navigation Handbook*, changes in barometric pressure will almost never account for an apparent change of more than 40 feet per hour at an elevation of 3,000 feet (a little more at higher elevations, less at lower elevations). Usually it is much less. According to Kals, changes in temperature can introduce much greater errors, particularly with an inexpensive altimeter that doesn't include some sort of temperature compensator. Even if it does, it's never a good idea to keep your altimeter in a warm vest pocket, then take it out and try to make an accurate elevation reading in 40° temperatures.

You can help compensate for these errors by periodically recalibrating over the course of the day when you reach points of known elevation. These don't need to be places where thoughtful rangers have posted elevation signs. As you hike, look for points you can identify on the map: things like trail junctions or locations where a stream intersects the trail, for example. Then check your topo map. You can get a pretty good idea of your elevation by studying the contour lines around your known location. If your altimeter no longer matches, reset it.

In general, you shouldn't use the elevation readout from your GPS receiver to calibrate a barometric altimeter. GPS elevations are significantly less accurate than GPS horizontal positions. You're better off calibrating your altimeter from your topo map.

Now that you know how to calibrate an altimeter, let's see how to use it in navigation. Basically, knowing your elevation gives you a handrail with which to work. On the topo map, you know you are somewhere along a line representing your measured elevation. If you can find the bearing to just one object on the map, your location will be the intersection of that bearing with the line of known elevation.

Refer to the illustration for an example. Suppose you have been cross-country hiking in the area around Freezeout Creek when the batteries in your GPS receiver fail. As you look around, you can see only one recognizable feature, a radio tower toward the northeast. Thankfully, you brought along your altimeter and remembered to calibrate it before you left. You take a reading and find your elevation is 800 feet. Next, you take a compass bearing to the radio tower and find it is at a true bearing of 75° (remember to correct for declination

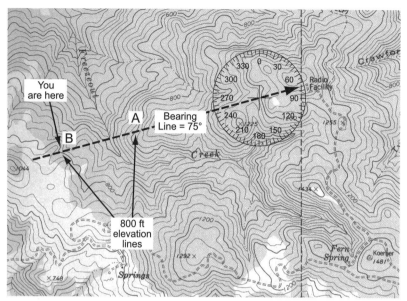

*When you know your elevation and the bearing to an object in the distance,
your position is at the intersection of the bearing line and your elevation.*

if you haven't adjusted your compass for the local declination).

Pull out your topo map, find the radio tower, and use your compass to plot a bearing line through it at 75°. Remember that this is the bearing from your current position to the radio tower, so you have to be somewhere to the southwest, along the elevation contour of 800 feet.

Notice the 800-foot contour line intersects the bearing line on either side of Freezeout Creek—once on the downslope and once on the upslope. With a little thought you realize your immediate terrain slopes downward in the direction of the tower, so you must be at the more westerly intersection.

Identifying your destination

Now that you know where you are, you're well on your way to getting back. Remember once again the Cardinal Rule of GPS Navigation introduced in Chapter 1: *it doesn't do you any good to know where you are if you don't know where you want to go.* Even without a working GPS receiver that's important to remember. Now it's time to figure out your destination.

Often this will be easy. You want to get back where you started. But this might not always be the best choice. It might be getting dark or you might be injured, and you just want to find the quickest way to civilization. Check the map for promising nearby features. You may be much closer to a paved highway than to your vehicle parked along a lonely forest-service road. If there's little hope of getting out today, look for a likely spot to spend the night: a ski hut, abandoned ranch house, or perhaps a sheltered cove with a natural spring you can use for drinking water.

Once you've decided on your destination, mark it on the map with a big "X." That way, in the heat of the moment you're less likely to get confused and start heading toward the wrong objective.

Planning the route

Now it's time to plan the route to your destination. Even if you intend to go back where you started, you might not want to travel the same route you took out. With a working GPS receiver you really didn't have to worry about the exact route to a destination; your receiver was always updating your bearing. Now, with just map and compass, you probably want to simplify things.

Unless you're really close to your destination, you probably won't be able to get to it in a straight shot. Just as you use GPS waypoints to create multi-leg routes, you'll probably need to identify several intermediate destinations. These could be things like stream crossings, ridge lines, trails, or man-made features. Make sure these are features you can readily identify when you arrive at them. You don't want to compound your problems by blindly hiking past your goal because you didn't recognize it when you got there.

Reading map bearings. At this point you have identified where you are, where you want to go, and the intermediate points along the way. You have one more thing to do before you begin hiking. You need to measure the compass bearing and estimate the distance from each intermediate destination to the next.

This is the same process as described more thoroughly in Chapter 3. Start with the bearing from your present position to your first intermediate goal. Lay the compass on the map with its direction-of-travel arrow pointing toward the first goal, then rotate the compass vial so that 0° points straight up (don't worry about where the magnetic needle points). Use the vial's north-south orienting lines, if it has them, as alignment aids. Then read the bearing as the number where the vial meets the bearing indicator. Now estimate the distance between points using the map scale and a piece of string. Write the bearing and distance on the map so you don't forget it. Repeat the process for each intermediate leg. Once you've done this, you're ready to roll.

Following the route

The first thing to do is go back and read the section titled "Common Sense Navigation" in Chapter 3. Many of the same principles apply here. Foremost is the caution against blindly trying to follow a straight-line route to your destination. Also remember the concept of navigating by visible reference points you've selected in the distance. And don't forget to triangulate your position occasionally as you travel and update it on the map.

Although there are many similarities, navigating a route by map and compass alone is a little different than using a GPS receiver. With GPS, you aren't so concerned about following a precise path because your receiver is constantly updating your bearing. With only map and compass, you're not so fortunate. Once you unknowingly get off track, there is no easy way to self-correct. And you *will* get off track; in the wilderness it isn't easy to navigate a precise bearing over any appreciable distance.

Aiming Off. Experienced navigators compensate for this by a technique known as *aiming off.* The concept is really quite simple. Let's say your objective is the one passable crossing of an otherwise dangerous river. From the map, you see the bearing to this crossing is

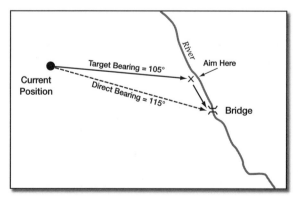

Concept of aiming off.

115°. If you try to follow that exact bearing, you will inevitably miss your objective, but you won't know which direction you are off. When you reach the river, do you turn right or left to find the crossing?

The question is more easily answered if you deliberately navigated slightly off course, say to the left of the true bearing. When you reach the river you might not know exactly how far it is to the crossing, but at least you'll know you need to turn right. How much should you aim off? There's no standard answer, but 10° left or 10° right is a good starting point. Decide whether to navigate right or left after studying the map to see which has the less hostile terrain.

Aiming off doesn't work so well if your destination isn't located along a suitable handrail like a river or trail. With a calibrated altimeter you can still attempt the technique by using elevation as a handrail, but remember that you can probably only determine your elevation to an accuracy of 40 or 50 feet. In this case you will want a destination that is readily visible even when you can only get within the general area.

Navigating Around Obstacles. Another thing you'll want to know is how to navigate around unforeseen obstacles. Even a 7.5-minute USGS quad with a 40-foot contour interval won't show you every potential obstacle. A ridge that looked inconsequential on the map might be insurmountable in real life. Or a normally placid creek might be swollen from recent rains. Either way, you need to take a detour, then get back on course.

Here's a way of doing it. When you come to an obstacle, determine the angle necessary to deviate around it. Navigate this new bearing for a known amount of time, then reverse your bearing for the same

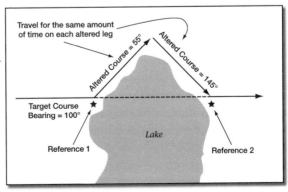

Concept of navigating around an obstacle. To improve accuracy, identify landmarks at both the near and far sides of the lake to use as references. When you reach the far side, sight from 2 back to 1 to confirm you are again on track.

amount of time. If you've done everything right, you will be back on
your original course.

Let's look at an example. Suppose you are following a bearing
of 100 degrees when you hit an ephemeral lake created by melting
spring snow. You have no choice, you have to go around it. After
studying the terrain, you decide to alter your course 45° to the left.
Your new bearing is then 100-45, or 55°. Set this bearing on your
compass and hike until you are sure you are past the apex of the obstacle. Keep careful track of how long you are traveling on this course
deviation. To determine the bearing necessary to get back to your
original course, calculate the complementary bearing: 100+45, or
145°. Assuming similar terrain, hike this bearing for the same amount
of time and you should be back in line with your original track. (If
the terrain is substantially different—say one leg is downhill and the
other uphill—use the method for estimating travel speed described
earlier in this chapter to determine when you have covered the
equivalent distance.) You can now set your compass back to 100° and
continue on course.

A second example will illustrate another thing to consider about
compass bearings: how to deal with math that crosses through a
bearing of 0° or 360°. Suppose you are navigating a bearing of 40°
when you come to a swollen river at right angles to your path. You
know your best bet for a safe crossing is to your left, so you need to
adjust your compass bearing left by 90°. Your new bearing is 40-90,
or -50°. Search as you might, you won't find a bearing of *negative* 50°
anywhere on your compass. Whenever you end up with a negative
bearing, you must subtract that number from 360°. In this case, your
bearing is 360-50, or 310°.

Similarly, if you were hiking a bearing of 310° and needed to
turn 90° right, your calculated bearing would be 310+90, or 400°.
Whenever this number is larger than 360, you must subtract 360
from it. So your new bearing would be 400-360, or 40°.

There are many other tricks of the trade used by skilled map and
compass navigators, but these are beyond the scope of this book. If
you really want to learn more, check out the sources listed in the references. But if not, don't worry. The concepts covered in this chapter
should be enough to get you out of difficulty when your GPS receiver
fails. Just remember they won't work if you haven't bothered to pack
map or compass.

11
Primitive Navigation Techniques

EVEN IF YOU'RE DILIGENT about preparing for disaster, there may come a time when you face a more difficult situation. You're deep in the wilderness, your GPS receiver is lost or broken, and you don't have either map or compass. Perhaps a bag got lost overboard on a canoe trip, or you've been separated from a companion who had all the navigation gear. Now what do you do?

The first thing to is to sit down and catch your breath. Don't let panic set in. Remember that generations of adventurers—Daniel Boone, Davy Crockett, and countless other mountain men—regularly traveled through virgin wilderness without so much as map and compass, let alone a GPS receiver. If they could do it, there's hope for you.

Hike out or wait for rescue?

You first have to decide whether it's more sensible to try to find your way out or whether you should just sit and wait for a rescue party. If you've been separated from a group or if you told someone of your plans and your expected return, you will probably be better off sitting and waiting, especially if you're injured or disoriented. Rescue teams lament the all-to-frequent story of a lost hiker continuing to wander like a moving target, almost as if he was deliberately avoiding rescue. Search efforts are conducted in a planned way, so if the hiker wanders from an area that hasn't been searched into one that already has, his chances of being found alive diminish considerably.

Once you have decided to wait, there are a few things to keep in mind that will aid your rescue. Rather than continuing to wander, put your energy into two efforts: finding suitable shelter and making yourself obvious to the search team. That way you're more likely to still be alive when you're eventually found.

Plan for the night well in advance. If the weather is bad, seek shelter under trees or rock alcoves. If you've got matches (you should *always* carry waterproof matches in the wilderness), start a signal fire. Even if people aren't yet looking for you, billowing smoke in a wilderness area may be spotted by a fire lookout or reported to authorities by others in the area. The fire's heat will also keep you warm during the long night. Just be careful about keeping the fire under control or you could suddenly find yourself in an even worse situation.

Self-rescue

If you know a search team won't be dispatched or if your party includes a seriously injured member who needs urgent attention, you may decide it's better to find your own way out. Without map or compass the task is more challenging, but not impossible. As you learned in the last chapter, there are four steps to the process: determining where you are, deciding where you want to go, picking the route, and following it to your destination.

At this point, most books tell you how to figure out where north is when you don't have a compass. We'll do that in a moment. But finding north solves only part of the problem. Similar to the Cardinal Rule of GPS Navigation, there is what I call a more general *Cardinal Rule of Navigation:*

> *It doesn't do you any good to know what direction is north if you don't know what direction you want to travel.*

So before you spend time finding north, ask and answer these three questions:

1. Where am I?
2. Where do I want to go?
3. What direction do I need to go to get there?

Answering the first question may seem impossible. Your initial reaction might be, "If I knew where I was, I wouldn't be lost." But with a little thought you should be able to come up with at least a general idea.

There may be times when it doesn't really matter. Hike for a few hours in any direction and you're sure to hit some sort of civilization.

If so, that's great. You don't need to know the techniques described here. But sometimes you will be in a situation where hiking in most directions will only carry you deeper into the wilderness. There might only be one direction that gets you back to civilization, and that's the one you need to follow.

If you really have no idea where you are and have decided to find your own way out rather than wait for rescue, one approach is to follow a stream or river in the direction it flows. It should eventually reach a larger river or lake, where you have a better chance of finding civilization.

Another alternative is to scan the night sky for the teltale glow of habitation. Just be sure you aren't fooled by a rising or setting moon. Mark the direction on the ground and wait for morning when it is safe to travel. (Night travel is generally not advised except in desert regions when the heat of the day makes travel impractical.)

If these approaches don't work, you'll need to gather your thoughts and list what you *do* know. The situation is similar to the discussion of dead reckoning in the last chapter. All you may believe is that you've generally hiked in a northwesterly direction for about seven hours, but even that's enough to get started. At least you then know that hiking southeast for a similar amount of time should get you in the vicinity of your starting point.

The techniques described below show you ways to roughly identify a specific direction, not always north. Some methods give you south, east, or west. Those probably won't be any of the directions you want to head, but once you know a specific direction you can sketch out a compass rose like the one shown in Chapter 3 to find the direction you want to travel.

A couple of words of caution. These methods work in the temperate latitudes of the Northern Hemisphere. Methods for finding direction in the tropics or Southern Hemisphere are beyond the scope of this book. Also be aware that none of these techniques gives you the ability to navigate with pinpoint accuracy. But they might at least get you within earshot of a road or visual range of a small town.

Celestial navigation techniques

Celestial navigation has been practiced for centuries by mariners sailing the world's oceans. Some of their tried-and-true methods are easily adapted for emergency use on land. These are the methods that don't require the use of elaborate tables or complicated math-

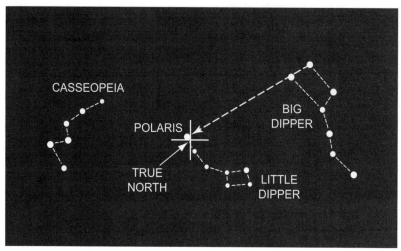

Finding true north from Polaris, the North Star.

ematics, neither of which is likely to be practical if you're lost in the wilderness.

Polaris. By far the most accurate method of finding direction without a compass is to use the stars. In Mexico, the US, and more northerly latitudes, the North Star, Polaris, is the easiest to identify. Polaris lies almost exactly due north, so close you can use it to determine magnetic declination. The easiest way to find Polaris is to first identify the Big Dipper. As shown in the diagram, the top of the Dipper points almost directly to Polaris.

In the late fall and early winter, the Big Dipper is low or even below the northern horizon in the evening, making it difficult or impossible to spot. At this time of year the constellation Cassiopeia, looking something like an upside-down "W," is a better reference. The top of the "W" points in the general direction of Polaris.

Orion. Another constellation many people can identify is Orion. The three stars of Orion's belt are one of the most notable features of the night sky. Orion lies along the celestial equator, so no matter where you are, it essentially rises due east and sets due west. If you have a reasonable view of the horizon you can see where it rises or sets and deduce the appropriate direction.

From about August through December, it's easiest to watch Orion as it rises in the east. In August, it rises in the early morning between about 3:00 am and 5:00 am depending on your location. In December, it rises between 6:00 pm and 8:00 pm. From late winter through late spring, it's easier to watch it setting in the west. The middle of summer is problematic because it rises after sunrise and sets before sunset. At that time of the year you would need to use other stars along the celestial equator as your reference, but that's a subject beyond the scope of this book.

The main problem with celestial navigation on land is that your references are only visible at night. You don't want to be tramping through unknown wilderness in the dark, so the best thing to do is mark the measured direction on the ground in some way—a line in the dirt or a series of rocks, for example. Then wait until morning to start moving.

Directions from the sun

There are several approaches to measuring direction from the sun, some reasonably accurate and others not. Here are three techniques, in rough order of accuracy.

Sun's bearing at noon. This approach can be quite accurate, if performed carefully. The principle is simple: by definition, the sun faces directly south at local noon. With the advent of accurate quartz crystal-controlled watches, it's relatively easy to determine when it's noon. South is simply the direction to the sun at that instant.

The apparent position of the sun changes most rapidly in the hours around noon, so if you want to be accurate, you need to precisely determine when local noon occurs. The sun moves through an arc of 15° every hour, or 1° for every four minutes of time. To find south to within 2° you need to take the reading within 8 minutes of local noon.

During the months of daylight savings time the largest potential source of error is forgetting to account for the time change. To figure out how to make the adjustment, remember the old saying "spring forward, fall back." During daylight savings, clocks are moved *forward* one hour, so when the clock reads noon, it's really only 11:00 am standard time. At this time of year, you need to take the reading at 1:00 pm, not noon, local time.

Throughout this discussion I've been using the term *local time* for good reason. Ever since the late 1800s the world has been divided into 24 time zones, originally driven by the railroads' need for consistent time at all stations along their routes. Each time zone is 15° wide, and the *standard time* anywhere within a zone is the same. The current time in each successive zone differs by exactly one hour (it's no accident that the sun also moves through a 15° arc each hour).

The sun, however, is not due south everywhere in the time zone at the same instant. Only at the longitude line down the center of a zone (the *central meridian*) is it due south at noon. East of that meridian the sun is due south earlier than noon, west of it, later. *Local noon* is simply defined as the time at which the sun is due south *for your current location.*

If you're at either edge of a time zone, local noon differs from standard noon by 30 minutes. At the eastern edge, local noon occurs at a standard time of 11:30 am. At the western edge, local noon occurs at a standard time of 12:30 pm. In between, local noon varies depending on how far you are from the central meridian.

If you don't correct for this difference, the direction you determine for due south can be off by 7° or more. Combine that with the fact your watch is probably not perfectly accurate and your measurement can be off by over 10°.

Correcting for local time is really quite easy as long as you know your approximate longitude. Find the difference between your current longitude and the central meridian of your time zone. Then apply the rule of four minutes time difference for each degree of longitude difference. Remember that if you're east of the central meridian noon comes earlier than standard time, if you're west it comes later. In the United States, the central meridians for each time zone are the following:

> Eastern time zone: 75° west longitude
> Central time zone: 90° west longitude
> Mountain time zone: 105° west longitude
> Pacific time zone: 120° west longitude

Here's an example. I'm writing this in Santa Rosa, California, located north of San Francisco in the Pacific Time Zone at longitude 122° 39′ W. This is 2° 39′ west of the central meridian for this zone. Round this to 2.5° and apply the rule of 4 minutes time difference for every degree of longitude to get a difference of 10 minutes. Since I'm west of the central meridian, local noon occurs at 12:10 pm Pacific Standard Time, or 1:10 pm Pacific Daylight Time.

A few other minor errors arise because the earth's orbit around the sun is not a perfect circle and its axis of rotation is tilted in relation to its orbit. These can account for another 2-3° error in your measurement. Considering that without map or compass your ability to navigate a precise bearing is pretty limited anyway, I wouldn't worry about trying to eke out the last degree or two of accuracy in your measurement.

You can slightly improve the accuracy of this technique by sticking a tall straight pole or stick vertically into level ground and noting the direction of its shadow at local noon. It will be pointing due north.

Equal height method. This method is based on the simple fact that the length of a shadow cast by an object such as a stick a certain number of minutes before noon is the same as its length an equal number of minutes after noon. With this method you don't need to worry about correcting for your longitude, and you don't even need to know exactly when local noon occurs.

You first need to plant an object like a stick, hiking staff, or ski pole into the ground. The surface of the ground must be as level as possible and the stick as close to true vertical as you can make it. At least 30 minutes before local noon, measure the length of the

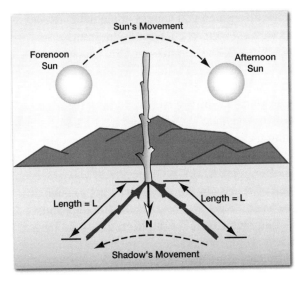

Equal height method for determining north. When the length of the shadow after noon equals the length of the shadow before noon, north is half way between the two directions.

shadow. Lacking a tape measure, you can use your belt or some fishing line, or even a fallen tree branch, to make the measurement. As you do this, draw a line on the ground to mark the direction of the shadow.

As time progresses, the shadow will get shorter for a time, then begin to lengthen. (If the shadow doesn't get shorter but continues to grow after your initial measurement you might as well stop, you've already missed local noon.) Keep measuring the length of the shadow as it grows until it reaches the same length you measured before noon. Immediately draw a new line marking the new direction. North is at an angle halfway between the two lines.

Using your watch as a compass. This is a popular technique reported throughout the literature, but despite the wide press coverage it's really not very accurate. It's based on the somewhat dubious premise that the sun is directly east at 6:00 am, is directly west at 6:00 pm, and is due south at noon. Assuming that to be true, then you should be able to use your analog watch to find south. (If you wear a digital watch, you're pretty much out of luck here.)

Here is the procedure: align your watch so the hour hand is pointed at the sun. This is easiest to do if you hold the watch level and place a slender stick like a match or toothpick vertically in the ground. Align your watch so the shadow falls directly in line with the hour hand. South is then halfway between 12:00 and the current position of the hour hand.

Recalling the previous discussion you should immediately recognize several problems with this approach. First, it doesn't correct for daylight savings time, so during the summer months you are immediately in error by anywhere between 7° and 23°. Neither does it take into account errors due to the difference in local noon from standard noon, or inaccuracies in your watch. The combination of these errors, even if you've corrected for daylight savings time, can exceed 20°, relegating this approach to last place on the list.

Other methods are often reported in the literature. If you observe the direction of the sun at sunrise or sunset you can get a rough approximation of east or west. To get accurate results, though, you need to apply a correction factor from a complicated look-up table that you're not likely to have in your pocket.

Another common but inaccurate method is to place a stick vertically on the ground and watch the direction the shadow moves. This gives you a rough indication of east. But because the sun describes an arc as it moves, the direction is only approximate. In *Land Navigation Handbook*, W. S. Kals claims that nowhere in the United States can you be assured of an accuracy of better than 20-30° using this technique.

Navigating a bearing without a compass

After you've determined what direction you want to go and where north is, you're ready to start your journey. Now the trick is to navigate that bearing without a compass. The lines you drew in the ground to mark north will be of no help when you're a mile away. And without a reference, most people can't walk a straight line for any distance.

A detailed discussion of the subject is beyond the scope of this book. But here's a tip you might find useful. It's based on the same "common sense" approach to navigation we described in Chapter 3, with an additional twist.

Pick a point in the distance like a mountain peak or distinctive tree in the direction you want to travel, and use it as a target. Your initial goal will be to hike to that target. Now turn around and pick another object *directly behind you* to serve as a rear anchor point. It doesn't need to be far away, it can be right nearby. It just needs to be something you'll still be able to see when you reach your first target.

Now imagine a tightrope stretched between this rear anchor point and the target object in front of you. You are the tightrope walker. Your goal is to stay on the tightrope as you walk.

In general, you won't always be able to do this. Undoubtedly there will be obstacles you have to go around as you hike. Make a point of getting back on the tightrope after you have gone around an obstacle.

You might wonder why you need to worry about tracking a rear anchor point. As long as you can get to your target, why should you care about anything behind you? The problem is that your initial target probably isn't your final goal. When you reach it, you'll need to pick a new target object ahead of you along the same bearing. But since you don't have a compass, how do you know what direction that is?

You could, of course, again use the primitive direction-finding methods described earlier this chapter, but there is an easier way. Look to the rear and locate your anchor point. Now visualize an imaginary line running from it through your current position and continuing forward. Pick a new target along this bearing and continue navigating. You may also need to pick a new anchor point. Continue going, selecting new targets and anchor points as you need them, until you eventually make it back to civilization.

When you don't have a map or compass, knowing how to navigate by visually tracking your surroundings can be the difference between getting to safety and finding yourself further afield in unknown territory. The time to practice these skills is when you still have a working GPS receiver, not after it's already broken. Whenever you are out with your receiver, consider using the techniques described here to hone your skills in visual navigation.

PART 5:
Getting the Most
from GPS

Key Concepts in Part 5

· Fun things to do with GPS
· All about track logs
· How to choose a GPS receiver
· Guide to receivers from popular manufacturers
· Essential GPS accessories
· Answers to common questions

12
Fun and Games

ONCE YOU ARE COMFORTABLE with your GPS receiver you'll un-doubtedly want to find new ways to use it, if for no other reason than to justify to the rest of your family why you bought it. In this chapter we'll give you a few ideas for fun things to do with your receiver, starting with solo activities and finishing up with team games. Don't be afraid to use these ideas as starting points to invent your own variations.

Track log maps

The previous chapters focused on how to use a GPS receiver to get you to a destination. But your receiver also excels at another task, that of recording the route you took to get there. Receivers designed for outdoor use all include the ability to generate a *track log*, or de-

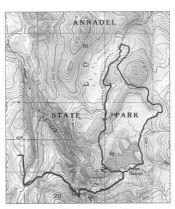

Track logs as displayed on the map pages of the eTrex (left) and Vista (center). At right, the eTrex track log has been downloaded to a USGS map using TOPO! software. This clearly shows how some park trails have been relocated from their original routes to reduce environmental impact on sensitive meadows.

tailed record of the path you took to get from a starting point to a destination. You'll often hear it described as a "breadcrumb" trail, in reference to the old story of Hansel and Gretel. But unlike poor Hansel's breadcrumbs that disappeared after being eaten by birds, your receiver's track log remains in memory until you explicitly delete it!

Track Back Feature. A track log can be valuable in many ways. In the simplest case, you can use it to retrace your *exact* path back to a starting point. (In contrast, following a waypoint bearing only shows you the *straight-line* path to a destination.) Simply activate the track log feature before you start out and let your receiver keep track of your path. Every time you pass a threshold in either time or distance from the last log point, another point is automatically added. This continues until you either complete your journey or the track log memory gets filled. Memories typically range from 1000 to 10,000 points, so even the smallest memory should be sufficient to record a journey of a few hours or more.

Be sure to clear your receiver's track log memory before you start out and keep your receiver turned on for the entire time. That way you'll get a complete record of your path without any extraneous information. When you are ready to return, go to the map page and zoom in enough to get a detailed view of the track. Then just follow the track back to your origin. Many receivers make the job easier by providing a "track back" feature that creates a route from your track. Your receiver generates a number of phantom waypoints from the stored track log and connects them just like any other route.

To create an accurate track log the receiver must have a clear view of the sky the entire time. This eTrex is mounted to the shoulder strap of a backpack.

If you're handy with tools, you can make a custom clip that allows you to attach an external antenna to your clothing.

Using a Track Log with a Computer. Perhaps more interesting is the fact that a track log allows you to store a complete record of your journey for future reference. Once your receiver has recorded a track log you can download it to a computer where you can display and analyze it on a software map.

When using a track log to create a detailed map of your route, keep several points in mind. First, for your receiver to capture an uninterrupted log you must leave it turned on for the entire journey. Make sure your batteries are fresh and always carry spares. You must also make sure your receiver doesn't lose satellite lock as you travel, so don't bury it in a pocket or backpack. Keep it out where it has a clear view of the sky and its antenna is correctly oriented. This is one situation where an external antenna is useful because then only the antenna needs to be out and visible. You can store the receiver safely in a case or backpack. I've had good success with a Garmin GPS 12XL and external antenna. I designed a custom clip so I can easily attach the antenna to my shirt. Purists recommend attaching it to the top of your head so your body doesn't block any of the satellites. Depending on your sensitivity to the "geek factor" you might prefer to put it in a less visible position inside the crown of a hat!

Another thing to remember is that a track log remains in memory until you explicitly clear it, so before you start a new journey, clear any existing data that remains from previous trips. Otherwise the old data and the new will all be recorded as a continuous jumble of information. You usually clear the track log from the setup page, although on some receivers you do it from the map page.

Finally, remember your receiver only has a fixed amount of track log memory. In most cases it takes at least several hours to fill up, but when it does get filled, your receiver starts overwriting the oldest data with the newest. (You can usually also select an option to stop recording when the memory is full.) The track log screen shows you what percentage of the memory has been used.

Some receivers let you move the active track to a separate memory. If your receiver lets you do this, you should store it when the track log memory approaches 100%, then start a new log. You can later download all the stored tracks into a computer where they can be joined and analyzed as a single record. This option isn't available in less expensive receivers that have only a single track log memory. Most receivers can record the track log in several ways. The most useful is the "automatic" mode where the receiver decides when your position has changed enough to justify adding another point to the track. Your receiver is smart enough to know that if you're driving on the freeway at 60 miles an hour there can be more distance between points than if you are walking a trail at 2 miles an hour.

You typically also have two other options: store points at either a constant time interval or a specific distance from the previous point. In almost all cases you are better off leaving your receiver set to "automatic" mode.

There are a few other points to keep in mind if you want to create the most accurate maps:

- Make sure your receiver is operating in 3D mode before you start out, and don't turn on tracking until you actually begin your journey. You don't want to record inconsequential track points as you wander around doing such things as loading or putting on a backpack, visiting the restroom, or checking in at a visitors center.
- Many receivers allow you to set the density at which track log points are added, even in the automatic mode. If so, choose the highest density option that will still let you capture your entire journey.
- Stay on course and avoid deviating to do things like admire scenery, make a pit stop, etc. If you do need to make a side trip, turn off tracking until you are back on course, and return to that point as closely as possible before you again enable tracking. Turn off tracking while making long rest stops.
- Watch the satellite status page as you travel. If you drop out of 3D mode, mark a wayoint at that location and another at the location where you reacquire satellite lock. The track log through this

region will be inaccurate, so you should make detailed notes as
you travel through it. You can later use these notes to correct the
inaccurate data.

- Mark waypoints at significant intermediate points such as trail or
  road junctions, switchbacks, or river crossings. This will help you
  later correlate your trip to the features on a map.

- If your journey involves backtracking and you don't want to activate the track back feature, you can either turn off tracking for the
  return trip or leave it on to get an idea of the repeatability of the
  track. If you do leave it on, remember that the total measured distance will be twice the one-way distance.

Using track logs, you can do such things as chart the course of a
river or design the route of a marathon race. These are fairly obvious applications, but there are others as well. I know one author of
hiking guidebooks who uses this approach to make accurate records
of trail routes and distances for his books. Another avid mountain-
biker friend used his GPS receiver to plot a 40-mile course through a
nearby state park. He then rode the course to celebrate his 40th birth-
day—and swears he'll continue matching distance to age every 10
years until he turns 80!

GPS golf

A good part of a successful golf game is knowing the correct club to
use for the current distance to the green. This is a great potential use
of GPS. There are many commercial GPS-based golfing systems you
can rent or buy, but it is also possible to use a standard GPS receiver.
You first have to store as GPS waypoints the positions of all the
greens and any other points of interest (sand traps, water hazards,
etc.). Then when you are on the course, simply use the GOTO function to determine your distance from the green or hazard. Remember
that most receivers report distance in feet, so you'll have to mentally
divide the answer by 3 to convert it to yards.

The roughly 20-foot accuracy of standard GPS is somewhat marginal for golf. Newer receivers with WAAS capability can bring this
down to a more acceptable 2-yard error or less—if you can lock onto
a WAAS signal. Fortunately, most golf courses are fairly wide open
spaces, so your chances of picking up a WAAS satellite are better
than average.

You might wonder how you go about storing the various waypoints. If you regularly play the same course, you can store the important waypoint locations during one round so you can use them in later rounds. You might also consider trading this information with others who have recorded different courses.

Find the flags

This is a group exercise I often use with students in my GPS navigation classes. It takes a little advance preparation but the result is well worth it. The exercise works best for groups of between 6 and 12 people, and you'll need several GPS receivers. You'll also need access to a fairly large open area such as a state or regional park that doesn't get a lot of traffic. (Make sure you use a park where it is permissible to hide objects for later recovery.)

The concept is fairly straightforward. A day or so before the game, one person—the *master of ceremonies*—goes into the park and hides a number of objects (I use small flags of the type landscapers use to mark the locations of sprinkler heads), being certain to accurately record their coordinates as GPS waypoints. The master of ceremonies should hide the flags so they are not likely to be discovered accidentally by strangers, while avoiding unwarranted environmental impact or hazards such as poison oak. On the day of the game, the group gathers at the designated meeting spot and the master of ceremonies hands out waypoint coordinates.

It works best if the group is divided into several teams of two or three people each, depending on the number of GPS receivers available. As a minimum, one person from each team needs a GPS receiver while the others should at least have magnetic compasses so they can follow the indicated GPS bearings. Each team competes against all the other teams to be the first to find specific flags.

For a group of 12 people I typically hide 10 flags. The group is organized into four teams of three people each. Each team receives coordinates for two of the ten flags plus a sealed envelope containing the coordinates of the final two flags. It is up to each team to program the coordinates into their receivers and go search for their two assigned flags. Only after they have found their assigned flags can a team open the envelope and begin the search for the final two flags, which all teams are competing to find. The first team to find their two assigned flags plus the final two flags is declared the winner.

Depending on skill levels, you can make the game more or less complicated. For novices, you should stick to a common datum and position format for all waypoints. For more skilled groups, you might want to list some waypoints in degrees-minutes-seconds format and others in degrees-decimal minutes format. You might also want to reference some to WGS 84 and others to NAD 27 (or even some exotic datum like Easter Island 1967 as long as you know it works in your region and that everyone's receiver includes it as a choice).

It's best if you can place flags at least 100 feet apart so that everyone isn't stumbling over each other as they search. You'll also want to keep in mind the athletic ability of the individuals. I typically place flags about ¼ to ½ mile from the starting point and assign the more athletic members of the group to find the more distant flags. Consider other details, too. The master of ceremonies is responsible for helping any teams that get into difficulty. Inexpensive two-way radios can be useful communications tools during the hunt and to help the master of ceremonies steer a team in the right direction if they start diverging from their goal. A prize such as a bottle of wine or picnic lunch at the end can serve as ample motivation.

GPS team building

Here's an exercise I sometimes use with company executives as part of a leadership training program. It is also useful for youth groups or athletic teams who must understand the value of cooperation. In industry, managers must learn that their business will only be successful if two things happen: each individual department must be successful on its own, and all departments must work toward a common goal. This exercise is designed to drive home both of those points.

It is somewhat similar to "Find the Flags." A group of between 6 and 15 people is divided into several teams of two or three members each. There must be at least one GPS receiver for each team. A reasonably large open space such as a park is also essential. A day or two ahead of time, I hide several objects in the park and record their waypoint coordinates. But instead of hiding flags, I use small plastic containers. The number of containers is one more than the number of teams—if there are three teams, for example, I hide four containers.

The last container is the ultimate goal. It is the objective that everyone is working toward. It might contain a small reward—coupons that can be redeemed for food, drink, or some memento of the program, for instance. Each of the other containers includes two things: the name of a second waypoint location and a clue to the location of the final container. Each team must find their assigned initial container, then go to the second waypoint. There is no hidden treasure at this location, it is just a meeting point. The idea is that all teams converge at this point and piece together the clues to find the last container. Only if each team is successful individually can the entire group reach the final goal.

Keep in mind that if you're doing this with GPS novices, you won't want to take the time to teach them the subtleties of position formats or map datums. It's best if you program all the waypoints into all the receivers ahead of time, then just give the teams the waypoint names and teach them how to use the GOTO function. The clues can then simply consist of parts of the final waypoint's name.

I generally keep the instructions fairly vague. Players learn how to use the GOTO function and they learn the location of their initial container. But they are on their own to figure out what to do after that. Part of the challenge is figuring out why you are at the second waypoint and what to do when you get there.

Make sure to program the coordinates of every waypoint into every GPS receiver. That way a team that has successfully found their clue has the option of helping another team that is struggling. Whether or not they actually think to do that is up to them. I normally wouldn't offer that advice ahead of time but rather let them figure it out for themselves as part of learning to work together. Once again, inexpensive handheld two-way radios can be useful tools to help the teams communicate with each other.

Orienteering: GPS relay race

Orienteering is a competitive sport in which you find your way as quickly as possible across wilderness terrain to a series of control points using only a map and compass. It is usually a solo sport where GPS receivers are expressly prohibited, although GPS-based events are becoming more common. Here's a similar, team-oriented idea that relies on GPS skills rather than map reading skills. It consists of a relay race in which each contestant uses a GPS receiver to navigate to where the next team member is waiting. It is particularly suited to runners, bicyclists, or cross-country skiers.

Start with two or more teams of four contestants each. Every contestant needs a GPS receiver. Well in advance of race day, the race organizer must design the course. City streets or backcountry trails work equally well. Unlike true orienteering, no topo map is involved.

Instead, contestants are given GPS waypoint coordinates and must use their skill and judgement to find the best way to reach them.

In designing the course, consider the type of competition. If it is a foot race, each leg might be a mile or two long. For cyclists, it could be 5 miles or more. Plot a closed-loop course—one that ends where it began. Identify three spots along the way at roughly equal intervals and record these locations as GPS waypoints. These will be the relay exchange points. Don't let any of the participants know these locations ahead of time.

On race day, each member of the team except the first contestant receives the starting and ending coordinates for his or her leg of the race. The starting contestant is given the coordinates for the complete list of waypoints. His GPS receiver will serve as the "baton" that is passed between each relay member. Its track log will prove that it traversed the entire course, so it must be cleared before starting the race.

Prior to the start, each team member must individually enter the waypoints for his or her leg of the race into their receiver. To make it more challenging, these waypoints should not be shared with other team members. Contestants then find their way to the starting points of their own legs, where they will wait for the handoff. Depending on distance and terrain, they may get there by walking, driving, or bicycling as appropriate.

Give the contestants enough time to get into position (15-30 minutes should be ample), then start the race. The first contestant must get to the end waypoint of his leg by following any route he chooses. If all goes well, when he arrives he will meet the second contestant and exchange GPS receivers. Of course this depends on both contestants having accurately programmed the waypoint coordinates and having accurately navigated to the correct position. Assuming a successful transfer, the race continues through all the legs until the final contestant reaches the finish line carrying the GPS receiver that traversed the entire route. At the end of the race, the track log from this receiver can be downloaded to a computer to confirm it got to all of the intermediate waypoints without shortcutting. After completing their individual legs, the other contestants can use the exchanged receivers to find their way back to the starting point.

To make it more competitive, different teams shouldn't follow the same route at the same time. If there are only two teams and the geography is uniform, consider having them run the same course in opposite directions. If more than two teams are involved, use staggered starting times.

Organized activities

You can easily invent variations on the above games such as combined events involving running, cycling, skiing, etc. Search the web for such topics as "GPS orienteering" to see what events might already be established in your local area. Geocaching is curently the most popular organized GPS activity, but new games regularly pop up on the Internet. For example, *geodashing* is a game in which a large number of waypoints throughout the world are posted on the geodashing web page at http://geodashing.gpsgames.org. The object is to reach the most waypoints before the game ends. Various other games can be found on the http://gpsgames.org web site.

13
GPS Receiver Selection Guide

THIS CHAPTER GIVES A BRIEF REVIEW of various GPS receivers suitable for outdoor recreational use. Equipment manufacturers are constantly updating their product lines, so before making a purchase decision, visit your local outdoor specialty shop to get current information. You can also do research on the Internet. A good starting point is the GPS information site at http://gpsinformation.net. It provides outstanding coverage across a wide range of GPS-related subjects. You might also want to watch or join the discussions on the GPS newsgroup site at news:sci.geo.satellite-nav.

The information in this chapter is restricted to receivers expressly designed for use in the outdoors, with emphasis on products for the North American market. It doesn't cover such specialty products as GPS wristwatches, receivers designed to work through a personal computer or PDA, or products intended primarily for marine, aircraft, or automobile use. I strongly believe that if you intend to make significant use of GPS in the outdoors you need a receiver specifically designed for that purpose. While it might be reasonable to use a PDA-based GPS receiver for vehicle navigation, I believe it's a poor tradeoff in the wilderness. You'll make large sacrifices in ruggedness, waterproofness, battery life, and ease of use. As both PDAs and their GPS attachments continue to improve, this might change in the future.

The receivers described in the following paragraphs meet the minimum requirements laid out in Chapter 2. Most will do much more. At a minimum, they can:

- Report your position in latitude and longitude or UTM
- Accept different map datums, including WGS 84 and NAD 27

- Determine your speed and direction of travel
- Store at least 500 waypoint locations
- Calculate the direction and distance from your current location to any stored waypoint and from one waypoint to another
- Plot track logs of your journeys

Garmin International Inc.

Garmin (http://www.garmin.com) is a long-established manufacturer of GPS equipment. They offer several product families for the outdoor recreation market, from the diminutive Geko to the full-size GPSMAP 76S. You'll find a Garmin receiver for just about every combination of feature set and price point. All of the products described here are true 12-channel parallel receivers that are waterproof to the IEC 529 IPX7 standard, which means they can withstand accidental immersion in one meter of water for up to 30 minutes. They are not designed for continuous underwater use, which wouldn't make sense anyway since GPS doesn't work under water.

eTrex® family. This is Garmin's current workhorse series for the outdoor navigator. The six products in this family range from the basic entry level eTrex with its bare-minimum feature set to the full-featured Vista. The more expensive members of the family incorporate a

eTrex Venture. (Garmin International)

thumb-operated joystick Garmin calls a Click Stick™ that provides a better user interface than the simple pushbuttons of the more basic products.

The plain yellow eTrex and its camouflage-colored equivalent are the least expensive members of the family. They don't have internal maps, aren't WAAS compatible, and don't include any additional features like magnetic compasses or barometric altimeters. They can store 500 waypoints, 1 route, and up to 1500 tracklog points (2000 on the Camo). The Camo also offers a few additional features like a hunting/fishing calculator mainly of interest to sportsmen. If you don't mind using paper maps and don't want to spend a lot of money, the eTrex is a reasonable choice, but bear in mind you won't be able to upgrade it if you later want more features.

Next lowest in price is the Venture. It adds the Click Stick, WAAS capability, 20 routes, and a rudimentary mapping capability limited to an internal worldwide city database and the ability to download MapSource points of interest. With only 1 MB of internal storage, you can't download road maps or topographic information.

The Legend, with 8 MB of memory, is the least expensive eTrex mapping receiver in the family. At a list price only $20 more than the Venture, most people find it the better choice.

The Summit takes a different approach. It doesn't accept downloaded maps or points of interest and isn't WAAS compatible, so it is more like the basic eTrex. What it adds are a barometric altimeter and electronic fluxgate compass. It can store 20 routes and 3000 tracklog points.

The top end of the eTrex line is the Vista. Its 24 MB of internal memory is sufficient to store street maps of a small state or topo maps of a large national park. Like the Summit, it includes a separate electronic compass and barometric altimeter, and like the Legend, it is WAAS compatible and can store 1000 waypoints and 10,000 tracklog points. All this capability doesn't come cheap—the Vista lists for about $100 more than any other eTrex receiver.

All eTrex products are small, lightweight, waterproof, and fairly rugged. The user interface is a bit spartan, with a minimum number of dedicated keys limited to PAGE, ENTER, POWER, and an UP/DOWN rocker switch. Models with the Click Stick are a bit easier to use.

eTrex receivers use a rectangular patch antenna (you can actually see it through the translucent cases of the Venture and Legend) that isn't quite as sensitive under heavy tree cover as larger receivers such as the GPSMAP 76 or GPS 12XL. Like all Garmin products intended for outdoor use, the internal memory in these receivers is not accessible by the user, so it isn't possible to increase it or swap memory cards. All eTrex receivers can connect to a personal computer through a serial port, allowing you to transfer waypoints, routes, and tracks in either direction, and upload MapSource maps to the receiver. As is typical of serial connections, data transfer is fairly slow. Uploading a full 24 MB to a Vista takes over an hour.

GPS 76 family. This is the "big brother" to the eTrex family. These units are physically larger with a correspondingly larger display. They have eight dedicated keys and a 4-position rocker switch that is used

to make menu selections. All three models are
WAAS compatible. They all use quadrifilar helix
antennas that provide slightly greater sensitivity than a patch antenna. They all also include
an external antenna connector and the requisite
serial port.

The basic GPS 76 is similar to the eTrex
Venture. It can store 500 waypoints, 50 routes,
and 2048 tracklog points. Its 1 MB of internal
memory can only be used to store points of
interest, not actual maps. The GPSMAP® 76 is
similar to the Legend. With 8 MB of memory it
is compatible with all MapSource products. The
high-end GPSMAP 76S has 24 MB of internal
memory and adds a barometric altimeter and
magnetic fluxgate compass, making it equivalent to the Vista. With their larger displays and
ability to accept an external antenna, these
products are a good choice for people who want

GPSMAP 76S.
(Garmin
International)

to do a lot of highway or marine navigation in addition to wilderness
exploration. The tradeoff is greater size and weight when you're out
on a hike.

Geko™ Family. The three members of this family are remarkably
small and light. They measure in at just under 4 inches high, 2 inches

wide, and 1 inch thick. At only 2.6 ounces, they
are less than half the weight of an eTrex. None of
the current Geko products are mapping receivers.
They are great for outdoor explorers but their
small size and lack of highway maps make them
impractical for in-vehicle use. Despite being so
tiny, they are reported to have satellite sensitivity
equal to or better than the eTrex family.

The Geko 101 is a very simple product with
a sub-minimum feature set and lacking WAAS
capability. It can store 250 waypoints and 3000
tracklog points. It has significant deficiencies in
that it can't create or store routes, nor can it be
interfaced to a computer. It might be suitable
for the casual geocacher, but it doesn't have the

Geko 201. (Garmin
International)

horsepower necessary for general outdoor use.

The next step up, the Geko 201, can store 500 waypoints, 20 routes, and 10,000 tracklog points. It meets what I consider the minimum requirements for general outdoor use. The current high-end model in the Geko family, the 301, improves on the 201 by adding a barometric altimeter and magnetic fluxgate compass. As with the Vista and GPSMAP 76s, these features add about $100 to the list price compared to the otherwise similar 201.

Rino° Family. The Rino, an acronym for "Radio Integrated with Navigation for the Outdoors," is a GPS receiver integrated with a two-way radio. There are currently three models, the Rino 110, 120, and 130. The GPS portion of the Rino 110 is similar to an eTrex Venture. It has 1 MB internal memory that can only be used to store points of interest, not complete maps. The Rino 120 is similar to an eTrex Legend, with 8 MB internal memory and full MapSource compatibility. The Rino 130 is similar to an eTrex Vista with 24 MB of memory.

The two-way radio capability is unique. Rinos can broadcast on both the free FRS (Family Radio Service) channels and the more powerful GMRS (General Mobile Radio System) frequencies, which require a $75 FCC license. The license is assigned to a specific adult, not a specific radio, and the FCC permits immediate family members of the licensee to use more than one radio to communicate with each

Rino 120. (Garmin International)

other under one license. Non-family members would need separate licenses. (Regulations sometimes change, so make sure you understand current law before using GMRS frequencies.) If you intend to use GMRS frequencies be sure to purchase this license, as unlicensed use can result in a fine of $10,000 per day. For more information, visit the FCC website at http://wireless.fcc.gov/services/personal/generalmobile/.

Canadian law does not permit the use of GMRS frequencies, so Rinos sold in Canada don't include this capability. If you purchased your Rino in the United States, don't use the GMRS frequencies in or near Canada. In general, check local laws before using any FRS or GMRS radio outside the United States, as many countries prohibit their use.

Rinos can communicate with any FRS or GMRS radio, so you don't have to buy more than one. If you do, though, you get certain advantages. Two Rinos operating on FRS frequencies can transmit and display their positions on each others' map screens, allowing you to track the location and movement of the other person. FCC regulations prohibit data transmission on GMRS frequencies, so this feature doesn't work in GMRS mode.

GPS 12XL. The venerable GPS 12XL, having been introduced in the late 1990s, is a bit of a dinosaur in GPS terms. But it is still in demand, so at least at this writing Garmin continues to sell it. It is larger and heavier than more modern units and lacks the ability to work with any MapSource products (it does have an internal worldwide city database). It uses four AA cells rather than the two cells in today's receivers, adding weight but improving a battery life to in excess of 20 hours. Its patch antenna is more sensitive than eTrex receivers, and it includes a jack for an external antenna. It also includes audible alarms, a relative rarity in current receivers. It is considerably more expensive than a similar eTrex Venture (which incidentally includes WAAS capability not available on the 12XL), so I can't recommend it as a new purchase. You can occasionally find one on the used market for a good price. Don't confuse it with the less expensive GPS 12, now discontinued, which didn't have the internal city database or the external antenna jack.

GPSMAP 60CS. (Garmin International)

GPSMAP® 60 family. The latest additions to Garmin's outdoor product line are the GPSMAP 60C and GPSMAP 60CS. Housed in a package similar to the Rino but lacking the two-way radio, they offer an impressive array of features: daylight-viewable color display, 56 MB of internal memory plus an additional 8 MB built-in basemap, and full compatibility with all MapSource products. The keypad is reminiscent of the GPSMAP 76. Like the Rino, GPSMAP 60 products use a sensitive quadrifilar helix antenna. Both offer what Garmin calls a dedicated geocaching mode that allows you to include hints and log the find for later download to a computer. Battery life is claimed to be as much as 30 hours. These appear to be the initial members of a family eventually intended to replace the eTrex series. Expect new receivers with black-and-white displays at lower price points in the future.

Magellan (Thales Navigation, Inc.)

Magellan (http://www.magellangps.com) is the consumer brand name for GPS receivers from Thales Navigation. If you've ever driven a Hertz rental car with the built-in NeverLost° navigation system, you already know about Magellan. They offer two series of receivers for the outdoor recreation market, the SporTrak° family and the Meridian° family. Both use true 12-channel parallel receivers that are waterproof to the IEC-529 IPX7 standard. All models include a serial port and are WAAS compatible. Unlike Garmin receivers, WAAS is always enabled and can't be turned off unless you know the unpublished and unauthorized button sequence to disable it. (You won't find it here—if you're interested you'll have to do an Internet search.) It isn't really necessary to disable it, since the receiver defaults to normal mode if it isn't tracking a WAAS satellite. All SporTrak and Meridian products use quadrifilar helix antennas that provide good sensitivity. They all have capacity to store 500 waypoints, 20 routes, and 2,000 track points.

SporTrak family. This family includes five models for the outdoor navigator. The user interface consists of eight dedicated pushbuttons (marked with symbols rather than words) and a 4-way rocker switch. The basic SporTrak, with it's bright yellow housing, is vaguely reminiscent of Garmin's eTrex, but it's really more similar to the Venture. It includes a built-in worldwide cities database to which you can upload additional points of interest with Magellan's DataSend™ software. It does not accept full maps. For that you need to move up to the SporTrak Map. This model includes a 2 MB North American basemap of major highways, parks, waterways, airports, and cities, and 6 MB of free memory for use with Magellan's MapSend™ software. The various editions of MapSend software include detailed street maps for US or international destinations, topographic maps, and nautical charts.

The SporTrak Pro provides   *Magellan SporTrak Map.*

an internal 9 MB basemap and 23 MB of free memory for MapSend data. If you are interested in topographic maps, The SporTrak Topo has a built-in 108 MB topographic database covering the Continental United States, Hawaii, and 80% of Alaska. It includes another 16 MB of free memory for uploading additional MapSend maps. Finally, the SporTrak Color provides a daylight-readable color display, 10 MB North American city and highway basemap, and 22 MB of free memory. It further includes a barometric altimeter and 3-axis magnetic fluxgate compass that provides accurate compass readings regardless of how the unit is oriented.

Meridian family. The Meridian is physically larger than the SporTrak and has a slightly wider display, making it a little more convenient in an automobile. Otherwise the GPS performance of the two families is similar. All Meridian products are mapping receivers, with one significant difference compared to either the SporTrak or any Garmin receiver: rather than using built-in memory they accept industry-standard SecureDigital (SD) memory cards with up to 128 MB of memory. When you change locations you don't have to connect the receiver to a PC and overwrite existing memory with new maps. You can store data on as many SD cards as you can afford and swap them out whenever desired.

The basic Meridian includes a 2 MB North American basemap. The Meridian Gold increases this to 16 MB, and the Meridian Platinum further adds a barometric altimeter and 3-axis electronic fluxgate compass. The Meridian Color, as its name implies, has a full-color display. It also includes a connector for an external antenna, but it lacks the altimeter and compass so it is otherwise similar to the Meridian Gold.

Lowrance Electronics, Inc.

Lowrance (http://www.lowrance.com) is well known for their line of sport fishing SONAR fish finders and their marine and aircraft navigation equipment. They are also an established player in the recreational outdoor market through their iFinder® line of GPS receivers. Although several versions of the iFinder are offered, they vary primarily by what accessories are included. Only two variations of the actual receiver exist. The basic iFinder has a 120x160 pixel, 4-level grayscale display, while the iFinder Pro incorporates a higher resolution 180x240 pixel, 16-level grayscale display. Like the Magellan Meridian, all iFinders accept external memory cards, in this case the industry-standard Multi-Media Card (MMC), that store maps from the company's MapCreate software. All have built-in basemaps and external antenna connectors. A unique feature of the iFinder family is its ability to accept interchangeable faceplates in various colors, similar to many cellular phones. One notable limitation is that the iFinder is not waterproof. If you're likely to get it wet, you need to put it inside a waterproof travel pouch that comes standard with the iFinder Pro. To address this concern, in early 2004 Lowrance announced the iFinder H2O, which is waterproof to the IEC standard. Models with a "Plus" designation include the MapCreate software, an MMC card, and a USB card reader.

Brunton Atlas. (Brunton)

Brunton

Brunton (http://www.brunton.com), a division of Swedish manufacturer Silva Production A.B., is more famous for their excellent line of magnetic compasses capped by the hallmark Brunton Pocket Transit. They were first to offer a consumer GPS receiver with built-in magnetic compass, the Multi-Navigator MNS™. Their current flagship product is the Atlas™ GPS, which is a Lowrance iFinder branded with the Brunton label. Additional mapping capability is offered though TravelZone™ cards that contain detailed regional city and road information. In all other respects the Atlas is similar to the basic iFinder.

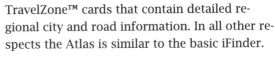

Cobra Electronics, Inc.

A relative newcomer to the GPS market, Cobra (http://www.cobra.com) is a well-known manufacturer of radar detectors and two-way radios. They currently offer two receivers, with additional products in development. The GPS 100 is a basic unit that can store 500 waypoints, 1 route, and 2,000 track points. The GPS 500 adds a joystick controller, 20 routes, 10 tracklogs, and 2 MB of internal memory for storing points

Cobra GPS 500. (Cobra)

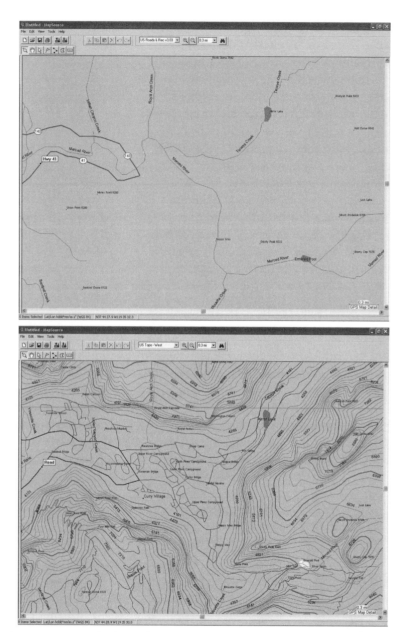

Computer screen displays of Yosemite Valley as shown by two MapSource products: Roads and Recreation *(above) and* Topo *(below). Either map can be loaded into Garmin's mapping receivers. (See Pages 31 and 76 for examples of GPS screen displays with MapSource Topo loaded.) Compare these displays to National Geographic's* Topo! *display of the same area on Page 104.*

of interest (not full maps). Both are waterproof to the IPX7 standard.

Cobra receivers claim one feature not available from other brands: they are 18-channel receivers. At first glance, it might not seem obvious why this is useful, since you only need to lock onto 4 satellites to get a position fix and there are never more than 12 satellites above the horizon. The advantage is that an 18-channel receiver is less dependent on having a current almanac. In almost all cases, at least four of the 18 satellites it is searching for will be visible above the local horizon even if you have moved hundreds of miles from your last position. While 12-channel receivers must go though a lengthy initialization process in this situation, Cobra claims to be able to acquire a position fix in about 50 seconds even the first time it is turned on.

GPS accessories

There are only a few GPS accessories I consider essential. Most important, in my opinion, is a sturdy case. GPS receivers are delicate pieces of electronic equipment, so when you are out in the wilderness they need as much protection as possible. You can use generic cases designed for compact digital cameras or a custom case specifically designed for your receiver. I like the hard-sided cases from AccuCase™ (http://www.accucase.com), as they are compact and lightweight but provide solid protection. They offer several custom GPS cases, including dedicated cases for the Garmin eTrex and III+, and a more generic case for various Magellan and Garmin receivers.

If you own a mapping receiver, you'll probably want to invest in the appropriate software mapping program from your receiver's manufacturer. That way you can load more detailed maps than available from the built-in basemap, limited only by the amount of receiver memory.

If you use your GPS receiver in the outdoors, you need a sturdy case. This hard-shelled case made by AccuCase is specifically designed for the Garmin eTrex series.

Both Garmin (MapSource) and Magellan (MapSend) offer several alternatives depending on your needs. You can choose from topographic, highway, or marine maps. With the right receiver, a highway map can guide you to an exact street address. Topo maps are great for the outdoor adventurer but can't automatically guide you to a destination. Since they are based on USGS topo maps, their road detail is not as current as a true highway mapping program. If you buy a topo program, make sure you know the level of detail you are getting. Some programs provide the equivalent of 1:100,000 paper maps, while a few offer detail similar to a 1:24,000 map. Page 172 compares the detail of Yosemite Valley shown by Garmin's MapSource Topo program with the same area shown by their Roads and Recreation program.

Brunton and Lowrance both use the MapCreate software, which currently covers highway and marine applications. Topo software is reportedly under development. Both also offer maps pre-loaded on 128-MB MMC cards. Fifteen cards cover the full continental United States and Hawaii. This is particularly convenient for extended trips where you can't easily upload new maps from a computer to your receiver as you travel.

To connect your receiver to a personal computer, you'll need the appropriate interface cable. These are custom designs, so your best bet is to purchase the cable offered by your receiver's manufacturer. You can sometimes save money by purchasing a third-party cable off the Internet, but the quality of such products varies widely.

Another useful cable is one that lets you connect your receiver to an automobile cigarette lighter socket. If you intend to use your receiver in a vehicle, you won't want to depend on battery power. Again, this is a custom-designed cable best purchased from the manufacturer of your receiver. You may also need to use this cable if you want to run your receiver from a 110 volt outlet. Most receivers don't offer a convenient way to plug into ac power, so if this is important you may need to purchase an adapter that converts 110 volts ac to 12 volts dc through a cigarette lighter socket. Then plug your automobile adapter into this socket.

Finally, an Internet search on the words "GPS accessories" will yield an almost unlimited range of products of varying usefulness. Depending on your intended use, you might choose to invest in such accessories as a bicycle handlebar mount, external antenna, PDA interface cable, automobile mount, training video, rechargeable batteries, or a wide variety of other software products.

14
GPS FAQs

THESE DAYS FREQUENTLY-ASKED-QUESTION LISTS, or FAQs, are all the rage. It would seem incomplete to offer a book on GPS navigation that doesn't include some sort of FAQ list, so here it is. Many of these topics have already been covered elsewhere in the book, but they are conveniently collected here in one place for easy reference. Some of the topics, ones of general interest but not essential for outdoor navigators, are covered here for the first time.

My GPS instruction manual makes it sound like I only need to track three satellites to find my position. You say I need four. What's the story?

To *accurately* find your position you need to be tracking four satellites. This is something many GPS instruction manuals don't explain very well. They might say something like, "With three satellites your receiver does not report elevation." This makes it sound like your horizontal position is still reported accurately. This is not necessarily the case. To get good results your receiver needs accurate elevation information. The fourth satellite gives it the ability to make that calculation. Without a fourth satellite, it must assume an elevation. The only one it knows is the last one it measured, but if you've changed position since then, your actual elevation could be considerably different. This can result in errors of a mile or more from your true position. When it is critical you know your exact position, don't believe your GPS receiver unless it is tracking at least four satellites.

Is my GPS receiver's readout of speed very accurate?

Yes, it is quite accurate, even better than the speedometer in your car. Contrary to what many people think, your receiver does not measure speed by calculating how fast your position changes. If it did, it would be much less accurate. It actually calculates speed by measuring the Doppler shifts of the satellite signals. It's the same principle that police radar guns use to determine how fast a car is traveling, and it has similar accuracy.

How accurately can my GPS receiver find my position?

Unfortunately, that's not an easy question to answer. It depends on several factors, some in your control, others not. The number of satellites being tracked and their locations in the sky are very important. Ideally, you want to be tracking one satellite overhead and three more spaced equally around you midway up from the horizon. Four satellites in a straight line is the worst configuration. Other error sources include atmospheric effects and the current level of solar activity (such things as sunspots and solar flares).

It's safe to assume that when locked on to at least four satellites, your GPS receiver can find its position to within about 50 feet. Most of the time it will be much better, approaching 25 feet or less. On rare occasions it may be worse. It is not possible to reliably achieve accuracies in the range of 10 feet or less without WAAS or DGPS.

Does GPS work under water?

No. Even an inch of water is enough to completely block the satellite signals and prevent your receiver from finding its position. Receivers are designed to be waterproof so they won't get damaged if you use them in the rain or if they accidentally get dunked in a lake or river. They can not find your position under water.

What about rain and clouds? Don't they also block the satellite signals?

No, water vapor or isolated droplets don't have much of an effect on the satellite signals (for the engineers in the crowd, the attenuation is less than 2 dB). The only thing you might have to worry about is if your receiver's antenna gets completely coated with water as a result of heavy rain. But in that case you can just wipe the water away and solve the problem.

Why does my receiver lose satellite lock under heavy tree cover?

Tree leaves are full of water. It's like having a solid film of water between you and the satellites. Depending on its design, a receiver may be more or less sensitive to this effect. A receiver with a good, high-gain antenna and low-noise electronics will do somewhat better than a receiver with a smaller antenna and less expensive circuitry. But no receiver will work well under heavy tree cover.

How accurate is my receiver as an altimeter?

The GPS readout of altitude is not very accurate, despite what you may read in Internet chat groups. Several factors come into play. First, the GPS system wasn't designed to measure altitude (called *elevation* in GPS language) accurately. The problem comes in the design of the satellite orbits. The details are fairly technical, but simply stated, the orbits are well-designed for measuring horizontal positions, not for vertical positions. The vertical measurement uncertainty is about three times worse than horizontal uncertainty.

Another problem comes from how elevation is defined. Topo maps and elevation signs report altitude referenced to mean sea level. Your GPS receiver measures it against a mathematical model of the earth. This model can be tens of feet different from true mean sea level in some areas. Overall, you can't expect a GPS receiver to measure elevation to better than a few hundred feet accuracy, and in some cases it can be much worse. If you want to accurately measure elevation you must use a calibrated barometric altimeter. Some more expensive receivers include a separate barometric altimeter just for this purpose.

How good is my GPS receiver as a compass?

That's a trick question. A GPS receiver doesn't really function as a true compass. Its "compass" page is actually an indicator that shows what direction you are *moving*, not what direction it is *pointed*. If you stop moving it stops working. It is really a heading indicator, not a compass. When you are moving faster than about 10 miles per hour, it does a very good job. Below that speed, electrical noise and system inaccuracies introduce more errors. It is still pretty good, though. I've never had a problem using the compass page to guide me to a hidden geocache, as long as I keep moving.

Some GPS receivers have a separate electronic compass built in. This is a true magnetic compass that is entirely separate from the GPS functionality. These types of compasses can find a bearing to an accuracy of 5° or less, similar to an ordinary baseplate compass. It's an expensive addition to your receiver and it eats up batteries rapidly, so you should still carry a separate baseplate compass.

Will my GPS receiver work inside a commercial aircraft?

It's possible. You need to be sitting at a window seat with your receiver pressed right up against the window. If you're lucky, the satellites will be in exactly the right positions and you can lock onto at least a few. (Even 2D mode is useful here since a mile or two error in location will still give you a good idea of where you are.)

It may take a lot longer for your receiver to get a position fix because you are traveling in the neighborhood of 600 miles per hour. (You'll see your exact speed when your receiver is locked on.)

A more important question is whether you are even allowed to operate a GPS receiver inside an aircraft. At this writing there are no laws prohibiting the use of GPS receivers in the US, it is strictly up to the individual airlines. Some airlines allow you to do so after the aircraft has reached cruising altitude, others prohibit it at all times. None allow you to operate it during the critical take-off and landing phases. Check http://gpsinformation.net for a current listing of various airline policies.

Does my GPS receiver send out a signal the government or anyone else can use to track my location?

No. GPS is a completely passive system. You can receive signals from the satellites but your receiver is not a transmitter. It doesn't broadcast any kind of information about your position. Like almost all electronics, though, it does emit very low levels of radio waves that could theoretically interfere with the operation of sensitive equipment nearby. That is why airlines won't let you use a GPS receiver (or any other electronic device) during takeoff or landing.

How is a route different from a track?

A route is something you create and enter into your receiver. It is a collection of waypoints you have organized into a specific sequence. When navigating a route, your receiver guides you from one waypoint to the next in sequence. When you arrive at one waypoint it automatically switches to guide you to the next one. Your receiver can only show you the straight-line path from one waypoint to the next.

A track is not something you manually enter. It is a detailed record of the exact path you have been following. When you activate the tracking function your GPS receiver automatically plots track points at regular intervals to map your path. There may be hundreds or thousands of points on a track, but they are not named waypoints and you can't easily read latitudes and longitudes of track points like you can for waypoints.

What is the "track back" function?

Many receivers offer a way to easily reverse your outbound track and follow it back to its origin. In this mode, your receiver automatically creates a route from its stored track. This can be useful if you need to closely follow your exact path back to where you started. This "track back" route creates a series of phantom waypoints along your original track that lets you return along your original route. Since a "track back" route consists of only a limited number of waypoints, it will not include all the detail of the original track.

Why does my receiver sometimes report fantastic speeds of many hundreds of miles per hour or show large, rapid variations in my position even when I am standing still?

This is the result of a problem called multipath error. You'll usually see this in difficult terrain like canyons, mountainous regions, or heavy tree cover, and in cities with numerous tall buildings. Your GPS receiver determines its position by measuring the time it takes for a radio signal to travel from a satellite to the receiver. This assumes the signal traveled in a straight line the whole time. Objects like mountains or skyscrapers can reflect the signal and make it appear to take a longer time to reach the receiver. If your receiver is picking up both the straight line and reflected signal, it can get confused and think you are moving very rapidly.

Why does my GPS receiver sometimes take a long time to find its position and at other times do so very quickly?

Your receiver needs two types of data to find its position. First, it must have a valid almanac that indicates the general locations of every satellite in the sky. Second, it must have valid ephemeris data for each satellite it is tracking. This is the very accurate information on a satellite's orbit your receiver uses to calculate its position.

Almanac data remains valid for about 6 months. As long as you use your receiver more often than that, it doesn't have to load a new almanac. If you let the almanac get stale, your receiver will need 10-20 minutes to load a new almanac.

Ephemeris data remains valid for only a few hours. It should take only a minute or so to load new ephemeris data from a satellite, and it can do this for all satellites at once. Since it might not start tracking all satellites at the same time, it could take a couple of minutes to load all the ephemeris information and find its position.

If you have used your receiver in the last hour or two, both almanac and ephemeris data should be valid so your receiver can often find its position in only a few seconds.

If your receiver loses track of a satellite at any time while it is loading ephemeris data it has to start over again. So if you travel under trees or drive under a bridge while your receiver is attempting to find its position it can take a long time to lock on.

What are the best batteries to use in my receiver?

Most receiver manufacturers recommend alkaline batteries as the best overall choice. Alkalines give good life and are relatively inexpensive. These are the batteries receiver manufacturers use to measure battery life.

Cost- and environmentally-conscious people sometimes use NiCad rechargable batteries. These are initially more expensive than alkalines but they can be recharged hundreds of times. Battery life on a single charge is very short compared to alkalines, typically one-quarter to one-third the time, so don't use NiCads in critical situations.

Nickel Metal-Hydride (NiMH) batteries are another form of rechargeables. They are more expensive than NiCad rechargeables but last longer on a single charge. Like all rechargeables, they discharge fairly rapidly over time even when not being used.

Lithium batteries are expensive and not rechargeable, but they can be useful in certain instances. They last about 30% longer than alkalines, but their real value is in cold weather. While other batteries quickly lose efficiency as the temperature approaches freezing, lithium batteries do a much better job of maintaining power. Here is a very rough comparison of the performance of different battery types:

Type	Relative Life Per Charge	Cost
Lithium	130%	High
Alkaline	100%	Low
NiMH	60-80%	Highest
NiCad	25-35%	Medium

Resources

Books

Kals, W.S., *Land Navigation Handbook*, Sierra Club Books, 1983.
Manning, Harvey, *Backpacking One Step at a Time*, Vintage Books, 1985.
Jacobson, Cliff, *The Basic Essentials of Map and Compass*, ICS Books, 1997.
Hattingh, Garth, *Outdoor Survival*, Stackpole Books, 2003.
Ferguson, Michael, *GPS Land Navigation*, Glassford Publishing, 1997.

Internet Sites: Equipment Manufacturers

http://www.brunton.com/
http://www.garmin.com/
http://www.lowrance.com/
http://www.magellangps.com/
http://www.cobra.com/

Internet Sites: Maps

http://www.topozone.com/
http://maps.nationalgeographic.com/topo/
http://www.maptech.com/
http://www.delorme.com/
http://www.oziexplorer.com/
http://www.fugawi.com/
http://topomaps.usgs.gov/
http://mapserver.maptech.com/homepage/index.cfm

Internet Sites: General GPS Information

http://gpsinformation.net/
http://www.edu-observatory.org/gps/gps.html/
http://www.gpsnuts.com/

Internet Sites: Geocaching

http://www.geocaching.com/
http://www.navicache.com
http://www.brillig.com/geocaching

Internet Sites: Land Navigation Practices

http://155.217.58.58/cgi-bin/atdl.dll/fm/3-25.26/toc.htm/

Internet Sites: General Interest

http://www.ngs.noaa.gov/GEOID/GEOID99/
http://www.usgs.gov/
http://www.travelbygps.com/
http://www.gps-practice-and-fun.com/index.html/
http://www.rand.org/publications/MR/MR614/
http://www.geolab.nrcan.gc.ca/geomag/northpole_e.shtml

Glossary

2D mode The mode of operation of a GPS receiver in which it is tracking only three satellites. Positions calculated while a receiver is in 2D mode can be subject to large uncertainties and should never be relied on when navigating in the outdoors.

2drms Twice distance root-mean-square. A measure of the accuracy of a GPS receiver based on the probability that the position reported by the receiver will be better than the stated number at least 95% of the time. Simple rms accuracy is similar but based on a 67% probability.

3D mode The mode of operation of a GPS receiver in which it is tracking at least four satellites and can accurately determine its position.

Agonic Line The line from north pole to south pole in which magnetic declination is zero. In the US, the agonic line runs from northeastern Minnesota to the Florida panhandle.

Almanac A coarse table of satellite orbital information stored in a GPS receiver and used to predict which satellites should be above the local horizon.

Baseplate Compass A magnetic compass consisting of a circular vial containing a magnetic needle affixed to transparent base. The preferred style of compass for general outdoor navigation.

Bearing The direction from your current position to your intended destination. Also known as an *azimuth*.

Breadcrumb Trail See Track Log.

CEP Circular Error Probable. A measure of the accuracy of a GPS receiver based on a probability the the position reported by the receiver will be better than the CEP 50% of the time.

Cold Start The process a GPS receiver must perform to find its position when it has neither a valid almanac nor valid ephemeris data.

Coordinates The alphanumeric description of a geographic location on earth. The most common coordinate systems are latitude/longitude and UTM, but a GPS receiver can be configured for many other choices as well.

Datum A model of the earth that describes it as an ellipsoid with a fixed origin and major and minor axes of specified lengths. The two most important datums in the US are known as NAD 27 and WGS 84. Strictly speaking, this is known as a horizontal datum, as opposed to a vertical datum which is used as an elevation reference.

Declination	See Magnetic Declination.
DGPS	See Differential GPS.
Differential GPS	A method that uses accurately surveyed base stations and a separate transmitter to correct for GPS errors due to atmospheric distortion. The US Coast Guard operates the most extensive DGPS system, but similar systems are operated on smaller scales by private companies.
DoD	United States Department of Defense. Operates the Global Positioning System.
EPE	Estimated Position Error.
Ephemeris	The very accurate satellite orbital information needed by a GPS receiver so it can calculate its precise distance from the satellite.
Fluxgate Compass	An electronic version of the traditional magnetic compass.
Geocaching	A GPS sport in which one person hides a cache and posts the coordinates on an Internet website. Other people use GPS receivers to locate the cache and exchange items in it.
Geoid	The line of constant gravity that represents mean sea level.
Geostationary Orbit	A satellite in orbit 22,240 miles above the earth, directly over the equator. At that altitude, the satellite orbits the earth once in 24 hours—the same time it take the earth to complete one rotation. So to a person on earth, a geostationary satellite appears to remain fixed in the sky.
GPS	Global Positioning System.
GPSr	Slang term for GPS receiver.
Heading	The direction you are currently moving.
Hot Start	The process a GPS receiver performs to find its position when it has both a valid almanac and valid ephemeris data.
Initialization	The process employed by a GPS receiver to update its almanac for the current time, satellite orbits, and geographic position when performing a cold start.
Ionosphere	The upper atmosphere of the earth, ranging from about 50 miles to 300 miles above the earth's surface. Ionized particles in the ionosphere cause a significant GPS measurement uncertainty that varies greatly depending on time of day and level of solar activity.
LAAS	Local Area Augmentation System. A system designed to improve GPS accuracy in the vicinity of major airports to aid aircraft during instrument landings.
Latitude	A line drawn parallel to the equator that measures how far north or south of the equator you are.
Longitude	A line drawn from the north pole to the south pole that indicates how far east or west of the prime meridian you are.

Magnetic Declination	For a given location, the difference in direction between true north and magnetic north. Also called magnetic variation.
Magnetic North	The direction a magnetic compass points. A physical location in northern Canada.
MB	Megabytes. A measure of the amount of memory in an electronic device such as a GPS receiver.
Meridians	Lines of longitude.
MGRS	Military Grid Reference System. A version of the UTM coordinate system.
Multipath	A GPS error that occurs when a satellite signal arrives at the GPS receiver from more than one path, typically because it has been reflected from a large surface such as a metal building or canyon wall. Because the two signals arrive at different times, the receiver can't easily tell which to use to measure the satellite's distance from the receiver.
Navstar	"Navstar Global Positioning System" was the original name given to GPS by the US Department of Defense. While it still shows up on official DoD documents, everyone else just calls it "GPS."
Neatlines	The borders of a topographic map.
NMEA 0183	The industry standard for communicating between a GPS receiver and a computer, developed by the National Marine Electronics Association.
Parallels	Lines of latitude.
Planimetric Map	The kind of highway maps sold at supermarkets and auto clubs. Planimetric maps don't indicate the nature of the terrain in any detail.
Position Fix	The process a GPS receiver uses to calculate its geographic position on earth.
Prime Meridian	The position of 0 degrees longitude. It is a line running from north pole to south pole through the Royal Observatory at Greenwich, England.
PRN Code	Pseudo-random noise code. The binary sequence transmitted by the satellites and used by a GPS receiver to determine the time delay between when the signal was broadcast by the satellite and when it was received by the GPS receiver.
Raster-Graphics Map	A software map derived from the scanned image of a paper map.
Route	A series of waypoints stored in a GPS receiver in sequential order. When the route is activated, the GPS receiver guides you from one waypoint to the next in sequence.
SA	See Selective Availability.

Selective Availability	The method once used by the military to artificially degrade the accuracy of civilian GPS. Discontinued by Presidential Order since May 2, 2000.
SIS	Signal-in-Space. Term used by the Department of Defense to describe the accuracy of the GPS signal as broadcast by the satellites and prior to propagation through the atmosphere.
Topographic Map	A kind of map that not only shows highways and man-made features, but also uses contour lines to indicate the shape of the terrain.
Track Log	The digitized record of your exact path of travel as stored by a GPS receiver.
Travel Bug	A geocache item intended to travel from cache to cache. Travel bugs can be identified by a bar coded metal tag attached to them.
Triangulation	The method used by GPS to determine position. Also the method for determining your position on a map by plotting the intersection of compass bearings to objects in the landscape.
Troposphere	The portion of the atmosphere closest to the ground. GPS error introduced within the troposphere is relatively small and predictable.
True North	The direction toward the true north pole, the axis of the earth's rotation.
USB	Universal Serial Bus. A relatively high-speed interface between a personal computer and a peripheral such as a printer or GPS receiver.
UTM	Universal Transverse Mercator. A rectangular grid used as an alternative to latitude and longitude to describe a position on the surface of the earth.
Vector-Graphics Map	A software map in which features such as roads, rivers, and topographic contours are stored as digital lines.
WAAS	Wide Area Augmentation System. An enhancement to civilian GPS that employs additional satellites and base stations to measure atmospheric distortions and broadcast correction factors a WAAS-enabled GPS receiver can use to improve accuracy.
Warm Start	The process a GPS receiver must perform to find its position when it has a valid almanac but does not have valid ephemeris data.
Waypoint	A description of the geographic coordinates of a particular location on earth, named and stored in the memory of a GPS receiver.

Index